A word of caution...

The recipes in this cookbook contain whole, real foods. It should go without saying that these recipes are in no way a "diet," but were instead borne out of a way of eating that reduces processed foods. I am not making any medical claims. I have no idea how your body functions optimally, so I'm leaving that part up to you—you are a grownup, and I assume you intend to cook recipes without sugars and grains. As with any new recipe, please read the ingredients carefully and consult your physician or dietitian before consuming if you have any sort of food allergy or medical condition.

EAT HAPPY

Cover designed by Telemachus Press, LLC

Cover and interior photos by Anna Vocino
About the Author photo by Joanna Degeneres
Back cover author photo by Matt Kelley
Author picture on page i by Andrea Anders

Published by Telemachus Press, LLC
http://www.telemachuspress.com

Visit the author website:
http://www.annavocino.com

ISBN: 978-1-941536-87-2 (eBook)
ISBN: 978-1-941536-88-9 (Hardback)

Library of Congress Control Number: 2017931676

Cookbooks / Food & Wine / Special Diet / Gluten-Free

Second Edition

Version 2018.01.06

Dedication

For Mom, who taught me how to hand wash dishes, set up my kitchen properly, and shop for spices. Because she was a United Methodist minister, I spent a lot of time at church potlucks, which are great places to learn how to eat. Mom dedicated herself to procuring the best education for me that she possibly could. She would most definitely correct me on the improper grammar contained within the title of this cookbook ("It should be an adverb, not an adjective," I can hear her saying). She apologized many times for passing along Celiac Disease. But without the gift of Celiac, I never would've begun this journey to better health. So thank you, Mom. For everything.

Acknowledgments

Thank you to the myriad ass-kickers without whom this cookbook would still be haphazard blog entries backed by empty promises. Jackie Fogel, Torri Anders, Daniele Passantino: you three gave tireless hours in the kitchen and at the store, and more importantly kept me on track when I wanted to quit no less than 6,000 times.

Thank you to the beautiful friends and family who inspired and contributed recipes: Jackie, Torri and Daniele yet again, plus Andrea Anders, Minnie Driver, Diane Evans, Leslie Tarquinio, Adrian Tarquinio, and Joann Neil.

Thank you to Matt Kelley for getting me down the photography path. Only a true friend comes with you all the way to Pasadena in the rain to make sure you buy the right gear from the camera store.

Thank you to Karina Allrich whose beautiful blog inspired me to track her down to meet her in person only to find a beautiful person who helped me and inspired me, even if she didn't know that's what she was doing.

Thank you to Jessica Gottlieb for your never-ending support, knowledge, advice, and generosity. I learned early on that letting you boss me around was the smartest thing I could do.

Thank you to Bree Melanson and Sarah Blondin for making me focus and being my accountability spirit guides. Even though you have the audacity to Skype me from places way more beautiful than North Hollywood.

Thank you to Vinnie Tortorich for barking at me to write this cookbook. Who knew that we would create such a fun community when you twisted my arm in 2012 to co-host a podcast with you? I adore the time we spend together on and off the mic, and I'm honored to call you a friend.

Thank you to all of the blog readers and podcast listeners. You guys nagging me over social media to get this book done actually cut the project time in half, believe it or not. It would've taken me nine years without your loving nudges.

Thank you to my food teachers/soul sisters: Haven Long, Jenny Andrews, and Nancy Carithers. All three of you taught me that maybe I should actually care what goes into my body and figure out how to cook it myself.

Thank you to my hands and hearts, who keep me balanced, motivated, and give me a sounding board: everyone listed above plus Jeannie Hayden, Nancy Wolfson, Lindsay Thompson, and Sarah Baker. All y'all sure do make a fine coven.

Thank you to my entire family, plus the two loves of my life, Loren Tarquinio and Lucy Tarquinio, aka the Ultimate Support System. Loren is the best recipe tester on the planet; in fact, I've never met anyone who can not only eat like you, but also convince women (least of all me) to constantly cook for you. Lucy, you are my joy rocket progeny who lets me be the kind of mom who does crazy stuff like comedy, podcasting, and writing a cookbook. Thanks for inspiring me with your creativity, sense of self, and fresh perspective. You are my hero.

Contents

My Story

In 1999, when my daughter Lucy was born, I went to my very first "alternative" doctor. He was a chiropractor who used muscle testing to see what types of foods were giving you troubles. I know it sounds crazy, but he told me my body couldn't handle gluten and to never buy cheap store-bought formula for my daughter if I could help it. I had never heard of gluten, and I thought he was out of his mind. He also told me to give up sugar and dairy for 60 days, as well, and for the first time in my life, my allergies cleared up. Naturally, the first question out of my mouth when he told me I was quitting gluten, dairy, and sugar was, "Well, what the F&*K do I eat?" Now this doc's methods may not have been traditional, but it was the first time I had ever thought that the food I put in my body was in any way tied to my health.

Cut to two years later, living in Los Angeles, where muscle testing and alternative doctors are on every street corner next to the nail salons. I got a phone call from my mother that her lifelong struggles with depression, skin rashes, and anemia, and her now routine blood transfusions because she wasn't producing enough blood were diagnosed as an auto-immune disorder called Celiac Disease. She told me, "It's hereditary. You have to get tested for it." It never struck me that I could have

the same thing. I seemed so healthy and energetic, like everyone is at 28, right? Turns out, I had Celiac, and it wasn't until I gave up gluten permanently that a number of chronic symptoms cleared up for me. Symptoms I thought were just a part of life: allergies, asthma, stomach upset, gas, bloating, diarrhea ... fun stuff, AM I RIGHT???

I was thrilled to know at such a young age that I could prevent a life of disease and chronic illness just by giving up gluten. However, I was sad that I couldn't enjoy the "treats" that everyone else was able to ... cookies, cake, pasta, bagels, pizza ... and I was determined to figure out gluten free options for all of my favorite comfort foods. I started a gluten free recipe blog with that vision in mind. Let's make donuts and lasagna that no one would know are gluten free!! Sounds like a good idea, right?

Although my heart was in the right place, my weight crept up. One of the benefits of Celiac is that I never digested much food, so I could pretty much eat what I wanted and be a size 2. But the drawbacks greatly outweighed the benefits (pun intended). Once my body started absorbing food and nutrients, I started putting on weight. And putting on weight. I seemed to always have an extra 15 pounds to lose. I wasn't comfortable in my own skin anymore. I joined Weight Watchers, but became so ravenously hungry after two days, I gave up. I repeated the same roller coaster on virtually every diet craze out there—the Master Cleanse! The Cabbage Soup Diet! The Zone! South Beach! I even tried Atkins, but failed after three days because I couldn't choke down all that meat and bacon (DUH, you need to eat vegetables if you're even gonna think about Atkins).

I just figured I'd buy the next diet book, work out a little harder, starve myself a little more, and then I'd finally drop the weight. I'd get down about three to five pounds and then would give up because I just didn't have the willpower to stick with anything. I'd go back to making my comfort foods and posting them on the blog. But I'd never post pictures of myself on the blog.

Then in April 2012, Vinnie Tortorich asked me to read his yet unpublished book, "Fitness Confidential." I was riveted by his hilarious stories and heartwarming life experiences. But I was mostly intrigued by his notion of giving up the sugars and the grains, what he coined 'NSNG.' I thought this was ludicrous, but I knew somewhere in the back of my mind that it would work. I dabbled in giving up sugars and grains for six months, and then went full force on November 6, 2012. The process of learning how to eat for a lifestyle choice instead of following a temporary diet took almost a year to unfold and become second nature. Now avoiding sugars and grains is very easy. I rarely miss them, and when I decide to have a little fun, I make sure I have only homemade treats with the highest quality ingredients possible. My taste buds are awake and alive now, and the physical benefits beyond giving up gluten have been too numerous to count.

I understand now that eating healthy, whole foods without spending all day in the kitchen is of utmost importance. I am a working mom who likes to have a social life. I need recipes that work for the family and are easy to make. Plus I need them to taste good as leftovers because who has time to cook at every single mealtime? I have developed, tested, and then retested all of these recipes multiple times over the past two years. Everything in this cookbook is from my kitchen to yours, and these are the exact recipes that I use on a daily basis to lose weight, feel healthy, and most of all EAT HAPPY.

Having spent a lot of 2014 and 2015 doing every known lab test recommended for someone with Celiac, I have discovered that I also have autoimmune reactions to dairy, eggs, and sesame. My way of eating is still evolving since I've locked down these recipes. Some people can have dairy and some can't (color me no dairy these days), and many of these recipes can be adapted to be dairy free. My next book will be sugar free, grain free, and dairy free for all of us who are realizing that avoiding sugars and grains is the perfect foundation for healthy eating, but that sometimes, our bodies tell us we need to dive a little deeper to find more wellness. If you have given up sugars and grains, yet you are having either an autoimmune or a hormonal issue, I highly recommend digging further. Finding answers about our bodies before we get sick is what makes all of this self exploration worth it. And if I can provide some yummy recipes along the way, then let's all EAT HAPPY together!

XOXO

Anna

Why Cut The Sugars and Grains?

There are a bajillion science books written by smartie pants people that explain the years and years of damage we've been doing to ourselves by eating foods with processed sugars, grains, and gluten. Go read those books to shift your paradigm, and then use this cookbook to apply a new way of eating.

What this book IS: I will show you how to clean out the kitchen, restock the pantry, shop, plan, and cook the meals that won't have you missing sugars or grains AT ALL. I've loaded this cookbook with veggie and protein recipes that incorporate great tasting fats to make sure you've eaten well and that you get full. I encourage you to experiment with the recipes, swap out proteins, substitute anything you like, have FUN in the kitchen. If you are out of onions, try a recipe with garlic and vice versa. Then write me an email telling me about your successes. This book is intended to inspire your mind to think of what to cook for you and your family in a way that is fun, creative, and most of all nourishing.

What this book is NOT: This book is NOT a diet book. This book will not make you watch portions or restrict calories. You will not be counting anything except measuring ingredients and how happy you are to be eating real food. I trust that you are a grownup, and as such, you can be in tune with the physical sensation of hunger, and on the flip-side, what it feels like to be full. If you are not eating sugars and grains, the only measuring you will do is sensing when you are hungry and only then starting to eat; and then to sense when you are full, so that you can then stop eating. This might be a revolutionary idea to some folks ... you know ... being all in touch with one's hunger instincts. I promise that once you've cut out the processed crap and add in healthy fats and real food, you're gonna feel like a new person. One who is in control of your food choices and your body, and that's one of the happiest feelings I know!

A note on sweet stuff:

I know a lot of low carb diets out there advocate using artificial sweeteners (Equal®, Stevia, NutraSweet®, Sweet'n Low®, Splenda®, etc.) to get you through those moments when you are having a sweets craving. I have not included any recipes that have artificial sweeteners in them. The sole purpose of this book is to teach you how to cook and eat real food. I want you to feel what it's like to go a few weeks at a time without eating something sweet and processed. If you decide to indulge, make sure it's not in response to stress, which causes you to eat garbage food made with crap ingredients that leave you feeling empty physically AND emotionally.

See to it that you are out celebrating life. Make your treats special, and make eating real food a daily practice. The sweetness of a strawberry can't truly be appreciated until you've gone without processed sugars for awhile. That strawberry will start to taste so sweet, you will hardly believe that fruit could taste so good. You will have a moment where you think the barista put sugar in your coffee when really you just taste all the flavors in heavy cream. Your addiction to sugar will be broken once and for all, and you will feel exhilarated being free to choose food based on what will nourish you.

There are a few recipes that contain some natural sweeteners in the desserts chapter. I have revised and refined my recipes tens of times to make sure the splurge recipes in the desserts section contain the LEAST amount of sugar possible to make the recipe work (and still feel like the homemade splurge that it's intended to be). If you are cutting the processed sugars and grains, a homemade grain-free dessert will be a delightful treat that won't derail your progress.

A note on olive oil:

If you care about food even in the slightest, then what I'm about to say WILL shock you. According to a yearly study at UC Davis, 69 percent of our country's supply of olive oil in grocery stores is not real 100 percent olive oil. It has been stepped on. That means that our beloved olive oil, the goldeny-greenish elixir that's at the heart and base of many of our meals, has been cut with cheaper seed oils like cottonseed, canola, sunflower and safflower oils, and sometimes even treated with chemicals to deodorize or to dye the oil so that you can't tell it's NOT REAL OLIVE OIL.

When I say to use olive oil, I mean buy the good stuff. There are nice Italian brands with a DOP certification, lovely brands from California, France, Spain, Greece, the Middle East, and Africa, but you've gotta do your research. Of course, I adore my Villa Cappelli olive oil, as I've stayed on their property and seen them make the oil with my own two eyes. All I'm sayin' is that if you are grabbing the first pretty olive oil bottle you see off the grocery store shelves, you need to take a closer look. Do not buy olive oil based on what's the cheapest or the 'lightest,' which is food marketer speak for "This oil has been cut with cheaper garbage oil to save us some money, but we're gonna make you think we're doing it for your own good."

In this book, when a recipe calls for olive oil, I mean nice, high-quality, 100 percent extra virgin olive oil. If there are other nice oils you prefer, feel free to substitute nut oils, coconut oil, or avocado oil, and the same rules of quality apply. As my friend Torri says, "Go make good choices!"

A note about soy sauce:

The second ingredient listed in most soy sauces is wheat. I cannot eat wheat because I have Celiac. And don't get me started on all the foods I have to avoid at Asian restaurants that don't cook with or carry gluten free soy sauce. So in this book, whenever a recipe calls for "soy sauce," I always use wheat-free tamari or gluten-free soy sauce every single time without exception. If you have a gluten allergy or Celiac, I strongly urge you to do the same.

A note about food issues:

The title of this book isn't EAT HAPPY, DAMMIT, AND THE ONLY WAY TO DO IT IS TO EAT JUST LIKE I TELL YOU TO EAT. The title is *EAT HAPPY* because I want you to figure out what you like to eat that makes you happy. I don't want you to have to count carbs or fat grams or any macros for that matter—or any calories or micros either, while we're at it. I want you to retrain your brain to love eating real food, to feel full when you ARE full, and to live your life free from the bondage of diets.

If you find that you are the kind of person who does better without dairy, then you'll find plenty of dairy-free recipes in this book, plus many more recipes that can be easily made dairy-free with a substitution or two. If you don't do certain kinds of nuts, I get it. I am highly allergic to macadamia nuts, so you won't find any macadamia nut recipes in *EAT HAPPY*. If you'd like to substitute macadamias for another nut, please feel free to do so.

The point is, this stuff is fluid. Do the best you can with what you've got in the fridge. Buy the nicest ingredients you are able to, or that are available to you, and have fun making dinner with your family and friends. Recipes are ever evolving, and I encourage you to substitute with whatever strikes your fancy. Then tweet me a pic because I love seeing what all y'all get inspired to make.

Pantry & Fridge Essentials

The following two lists contain a shopping list for most of the items that recur in this cookbook. You can slowly build up the pantry items as they tend to be more expensive, but they last for several meals. As for the perishables, this second list gives you an idea of what your weekly grocery list might be, which will enable you to make a variety of the recipes in this book.

Please note: whenever financially possible and physically available, choose organic fruits and vegetables, free range poultry and eggs, wild caught salmon, and grass fed beef. It can't hurt to avoid excess pesticides, GMOs, hormones, antibiotics, additives, fillers and anything else that makes our food unnatural.

Pantry Essentials

Chicken bouillon and/or broth (you can also make your own and freeze it)
Raw almonds
Almond meal/almond flour (these can be used interchangeably)
Coconut flour
Coconut flakes
Coconut oil
Cacao bars
Gluten-free soy sauce or tamari
Sea salt
Fresh pepper grinder
Garlic powder
Onion powder
Chili powder
Cumin
Cinnamon
GF Worcestershire sauce
gloves

Chinese five spice
Dried basil
Dried thyme
Dried oregano
Balsamic vinegar
Dijon mustard
Olive oil (get the good kind, and always extra virgin)
Rice wine vinegar
Champagne vinegar
Red wine vinegar
Cans of coconut milk/cream
Cans of diced tomatoes
Tomato paste
Some types of beans if you enjoy beans (I like cannellini beans, black beans, lentils, and pinto beans)
apple cider vinegar

Stock The Fridge

Your favorite lettuce (mine are red leaf and butter lettuce)
Broccoli
Spinach
Kale
Zucchini
Cauliflower
Onions
Peppers (I like the bags of small sweet peppers that are easy to cut and cook)
Whole milk
Heavy cream
Crème fraîche
Cream cheese
Coconut or almond milk/cream for the dairy-free people
garlic

A big wedge of fresh parmesan
Eggs
Bacon
Prosciutto and/or salami
Apples, peaches, pears
Berries (fresh when they're in season, frozen when they're not)
Your favorite proteins: chicken, pork, fish, etc.
Avocados
Lemons and limes
Tomatoes
Fresh herbs: basil, sage, thyme, rosemary, mint, cilantro, etc.

WOW, that's a huge grocery list. Well, you don't have to buy everything all at once. Sign up at www.annavocino.com for additional recipes, 4 weeks of suggested meal plans from EAT HAPPY, and other shopping tips and bonuses.

spatula
whisk
saute pan non stick
skillet
large
paper towels
baggies/pastry bag
food processor Vitamix/blender
mixing bowls
parchment paper
8 x 8 baking pan glass
9 x 12 -
fridge/freezer airtight container
pizza cutter
baking sheet
Le Creuset, dutch oven, slow cooker
plastic wrap
cheese cloth
cast iron skillet
aluminum foil my Trick
pastry brush
bamboo skewers
grill pan/cast iron
shallow bowl for dredging
roasting pan/pyrex
slotted spoon
large salad bowl
deep casserole dish
spiralizer

instant read thermometer
4 x 8 loaf pan (9)
9 x 9 baking dish (9z)
big stock pot or cast iron
mandoline
ramekins - 4 or 6
broiler proof
broiler rack
immersion blender
wooden spoon
colander/strainer
vegetable peeler
box grater
hand mixer
soft rubber spatula
muffin tin x 2 (200)
metal bowl
spring form pan
pie plate
custard cups
gloves

Izzy the Italian Greyhound very much wants salmon scraps.

Chapter One: Starters and Snacks

Super Guac!

(Serves 4–8)

4–6 avocados
1 small vine-ripened tomato, diced
Juice of 1 lime
2 tablespoons cilantro, finely chopped
1 small shallot, finely diced
1/2 serrano pepper, finely diced
Salt and pepper to taste

Combine all of the ingredients folding with a spatula, then whisking, but don't over mix. You can substitute to your heart's desire—jalapeño for the serrano pepper, go lighter on the cilantro, whatever your personal guac preferences are. You can even use lemon juice if you don't have a lime available.

Smoked Salmon with Coconut Flour Blini

(Yield 22-25 blini)

'Blini' is the fancy Russian word for mini buckwheat pancakes, but we all know pancakes are one of the first things we say our goodbyes to when we cut out grains. Buckwheat gets a bad rap, even though it's one of the lowest carb grains out there. It's still a grain; and we're doing this thing without grains, aren't we?

So howsabout we make grain-free pancakes and we slap on some crème fraîche, smoked salmon, and dill sprigs, and call said pancakes blini? I think we can all get on board with that.

1/2 cup coconut flour
1/2 teaspoon baking powder
1/2 teaspoon salt
3 eggs
2 tablespoons butter, melted, plus additional butter for cooking
3/4 cup milk
Crème fraîche for serving
4 ounces smoked salmon
Fresh dill, separated into sprigs

In a medium mixing bowl, whisk together coconut flour, baking powder, and salt. Add eggs, stirring lightly until dough is lumpy. Add in melted butter. Stir in milk, 1/4 cup at a time until batter is the consistency of a thick pancake batter.

Heat a pat of butter in a sauté pan to medium high heat until pan is very hot and butter is starting to brown. Starting at 12 o'clock on the pan, scoop a teaspoon of batter onto the hot pan, using the teaspoon to flatten the batter into a mini-pancake. Repeat clockwise around the sauté pan. Cook for about 2 minutes, flip blini, then cook for another 1-2 minutes on the other side. Let cool on a paper towel lined plate. Repeat with more butter in the hot pan until all the batter is made into blini.

Place the cooled blini on a serving tray, then put a dollop of crème fraîche on each of the blini, top with some smoked salmon and a sprig of fresh dill. Serve with an ice-cold martini or soda water with lime.

Prosciutto Wrapped Peaches

(Yield 16-18 pieces)

At holiday time, people will be dropping by. Even when it's not holiday time, people will be dropping by. People have a way of dropping by.

The people will require cocktails. Then they will require food to go with said cocktails. Keep a package of nice prosciutto in the fridge, wrap it around any fruit you have on hand (peeled, please), and fry it up in a hot pan. Your guests will think you are a savory-sweet wizard. I love peaches, but I've also used melon, figs, oranges, apples, grapefruits, and plums, depending on what's available.

Bring on the people! I am ready.

3 peaches, peeled, pitted, and cut into 1-inch wedges
5 slices of prosciutto, sliced lengthwise and into thirds

Wrap prosciutto around peach slices, using a toothpick to keep in place if necessary.

Heat a sauté pan to medium high heat, place prosciutto wrapped peaches in a clock formation in your pan, starting with the twelve o'clock position. This way you remember where you started when it's time to flip each piece. Cook until prosciutto is hardening, but is not too crisp. Flip and repeat on each side of the peach wedge. The peach will be warm and slightly gooey on the outside. Serve immediately. Watch your guests "ooh" and "ahh" as the peaches melt in their mouths.

CHEESE CRISPS

(Yield 1 crisp)

Sometimes we miss crispy, crunchy foods when we've forsaken processed grains, but these cheese crisps take the place of a good cracker or chip, with the added bonus of being more filling and lower in carbs.

1/4 cup shredded cheese (cheddar, mozzarella, or Colby Jack)

Heat a small sauté pan to medium high heat, spread shredded cheese into a 4-6" circle and fry in pan, being careful not to burn, until cheese is golden and bubbly. Remove from pan and let cool on a paper towel. Or eat immediately, but please don't burn your mouth.

Alternately, place 1/4 cup shredded cheese on a plate. Spread thinly into a 4-6" circle. Microwave 75-90 seconds until the cheese comes out in a cooked, flat disk. Peel the cheese crisp off the plate and let cool until crispy.

Tzatziki Dip

(Yield 2.5 cups)

5 Persian cucumbers or
1 large English cucumber, roughly peeled and chopped
1 tablespoon fresh dill, chopped
1 garlic clove, chopped
2 tablespoons lemon juice (about 1/2 a lemon)
2 teaspoons salt
2 cups Greek yogurt
Salt and pepper for finishing

Lay cucumber pieces on a flat surface. Sprinkle with salt and let sit for 10 minutes to draw out excess water. Dab dry with a paper towel. Combine dill, garlic, cucumber, lemon juice, and salt in a food processor or Vitamix®. Pulse until blended but chunky. Pour into a mixing bowl. Whisk in Greek yogurt, combining well. Serve alongside grilled meat and veggies, or as a dip with Almond Flour Pita Chips (see p.10).

ALMOND FLOUR PITA CHIPS

(Serves 2-4)

1 1/2 cups almond flour, plus extra for dusting on rolling pin to prevent sticking
1/2 teaspoon garlic powder
1/2 teaspoon salt
1 egg

Preheat oven to 350°. Whisk together almond flour, garlic powder, and salt. Add egg and mix together well into a thick batter. Roll or press batter out evenly onto parchment paper to approximately 1/4-inch thickness. Bake for 15 minutes or until crisp and golden brown. Break apart into chips.

Sausage Stuffed Mushrooms

(Serves 8–10)

Yummy little hors d'oeuvres ... that's what a party is all about. Trying to keep from eating all the stuffed mushrooms before the party starts, that's what willpower is all about. If you choose a very fatty sausage, you might find you need to drain off the fat after you've browned the sausage, before you add in the red wine vinegar. The last thing we want is anything too greasy. We want fat, not grease. (That's what she said.)

2 tablespoons olive oil
1 small onion, finely chopped
1 garlic clove, minced
1 pound of large button or baby bella mushrooms, stems cored out and finely chopped for the stuffing mixture
1 pound of your favorite sausage, casing discarded
1 tablespoon red wine vinegar
2/3 cup almond flour, plus more for sprinkling
1/4 cup of Boursin cheese (the original firm cheese, not the spread)

Preheat oven to 325°. In a large sauté pan with olive oil heated to medium high heat, cook onion until soft, about 3–4 minutes. Add garlic, cook another 1 minute. Add chopped mushroom stems. Cook 4–5 minutes until very soft. Add sausage, browning thoroughly and using spatula to chop up into small bits. Drain and discard excess fat if necessary. Sprinkle red wine vinegar over sausage. Mix in almond flour evenly. Remove from heat and fold in Boursin cheese until evenly mixed and creamy.

Place mushroom caps hollow side up in an 8 x 8 baking pan. Spoon sausage mixture into mushroom caps. Sprinkle additional almond flour on top.

Bake at 325° for 45 minutes, or until mushrooms are cooked and topping is golden brown. Cool for 10 minutes, then serve.

Kalamata Olive Tapenade

(Yield 2.5 cups)

One of the most versatile spreads, olive tapenade is a savory lover's dream. It adds flavor and flair to any appetizer spread, plus you can use it as a component in a number of mains and sides. Serve with raw veggies, place a dollop on your zucchini pasta, or alongside tzatziki and almond flour pita chips. You can also smear some onto your grilled steak, rub under the skin of your chicken before you roast it, add it to hummus, or lay a dollop into your turkey rollups.

1/3 cup raw pine nuts
2 cups pitted kalamata olives
2 tablespoons capers, rinsed off
2 teaspoons Dijon mustard
1/2 teaspoon minced garlic
2 tablespoons olive oil
1 teaspoon fresh lemon juice
2 anchovy fillets, rinsed and dried (optional)

In a food processor, blend the pine nuts until they turn into a nut butter, about 30–45 seconds. Add the remaining ingredients and pulse until finely chopped, with a chunky paste consistency, about 10 pulses, scraping down the side of the food processor to make sure all ingredients blend nicely.

Put in airtight container and refrigerate overnight to let the flavors really settle in. Bring to room temperature before serving.

Cheese Biscuits/Cheese Straws
(Same ingredients, different presentation)
(Yields 12 biscuits)

Luncheons, teas, weddings, funerals, Fourth of July, or holiday parties, in the South we serve cheese biscuits or cheese straws at every social event. In fact, if you are really into embarrassing yourself, throw a party in Atlanta, invite a lot of old biddies, and dare NOT to serve cheese biscuits or straws. See how fast your social standing plummets. I would hate to see that happen to any of us. Here is a low carb version of cheese biscuits/cheese straws that will keep your social standing well in tact.

1/2 cup almond flour
1/4 teaspoon sea salt
1/8 teaspoon garlic powder
1 egg
2 tablespoons butter, melted
2 cups extra sharp cheddar cheese, shredded and chopped finely
1/8 teaspoon cayenne (optional)

Preheat oven to 400°. Mix almond flour, sea salt, garlic powder, egg, melted butter, shredded cheddar, and cayenne in a large mixing bowl until a dough forms.

On a parchment paper lined baking sheet, spoon or scoop 1-inch balls of dough placed a few inches apart. Bake in oven 15 minutes, or until golden in color. Serve hot, or let cool completely, then serve.

Alternative instructions for Cheese Straws:

Mix the dough as instructed above. Spread dough evenly into a parchment lined 8 x 8 glass baking dish. Using a pizza cutter, pre-score the dough once in the middle horizontally, then 1 inch apart parallel lines. Bake in oven 15 minutes, or until golden in color. Carefully remove from pan. Using your pizza cutter again, separate the cheese straws into strips, let cool completely, then serve.

KALE CHIPS

(Serves 2)

1 bunch of kale
2 tablespoons olive oil
1 tablespoon white balsamic vinegar
1 teaspoon salt
1/4 teaspoon pepper
1/2 teaspoon garlic salt
1/4 teaspoon smoked paprika
1/8 teaspoon cayenne pepper (optional, for kick)

Preheat oven to 250°. Wash kale, cut out and discard hard center stem, cut kale into pieces. In a large bowl, rub kale with olive oil and vinegar. Line a baking sheet with parchment paper, spread kale out evenly in a single layer. Bake for 40 minutes, flipping kale at least once to avoid burning. In a separate bowl, whisk together spices. Remove kale from oven and season with spice mix as desired.

DEVILED EGGS WITH GREEK YOGURT

(Yield 24 deviled egg halves)

12 eggs, boiled, cooled, and peeled
1/3 cup full fat Greek yogurt
1 teaspoon olive oil
1/2 teaspoon salt
1/4 teaspoon pepper
1 tablespoon Dijon mustard
1 green onion, finely chopped

Hard boil eggs for 10 minutes, drain water, let cool for 30 minutes and gently peel. Slice eggs in half. Pop yolks out of egg whites and into a mixing bowl. Add the Greek yogurt, olive oil, salt, pepper, Dijon mustard, and green onion. Evenly mix ingredients until smooth.

If you wanna be fancy, scoop the yolk mixture into a plastic baggie (or pastry bag), trim off the corner and pipe into the egg whites evenly. Otherwise spoon the yolk mixture back into the egg whites evenly. Keep stored in the fridge until served.

Cheese Stuffed Mini Peppers

(Yield 20-24)

1 bag of mini bell peppers
1 package of Boursin cheese
1 bunch of fresh green herbs, such as chives, basil, or parsley, finely chopped

Preheat oven to 350°. Prep peppers by washing and cutting off top 1/2-inch (the part with the stem), then cutting in half. Scoop out any remaining seeds. Stuff the pepper halves level with Boursin cheese. Place on baking sheet and bake in oven for 15 minutes, or until starting to brown on top. Remove from oven, sprinkle with fresh herbs, and serve immediately.

Broccoli Dip

(Yield 1.5-2 cups)

Dips are fun. Whip up a dip, get some friends over, pour some cocktails, and you have an instant party. I like this broccoli dip because I'd usually see something like this served in a bread bowl, which means gluten contamination, which means no dip for me. So I control the dip environment by making my own and serving it in a bowl alongside some fresh veggies.

Cooking note: If you prefer, you can steam the broccoli on the stovetop, but if you're in a rush before a party and want to save a step, you can microwave instead.

---

1 bag of broccoli florets (usually about 12-14 ounces)
1 medium shallot, minced
1/2 teaspoon minced garlic
2/3 cup mayonnaise
2/3 cup Greek yogurt
Pinch of salt
A few cracks of fresh pepper
1/8 teaspoon ground cayenne pepper (optional, for a kick)

Microwave the bag of broccoli florets on high for 4 minutes. Pour into a bowl to cool. In food processor or Vitamix® pour shallots, garlic, mayonnaise, Greek yogurt, salt, pepper, and cayenne. Blend for about 20 seconds, then add the broccoli and pulse 5 or 6 times until broccoli is finely chopped.

BACON WRAPPED DATES

(Yield 25-30)

25-30 Medjool dates, pitted
1 pound applewood smoked bacon or
any other kind of nitrate-free thick bacon, at room temperature
Goat cheese (optional)
Toothpicks

Preheat oven to 400°.

Slice bacon strips in half lengthwise. If using goat cheese, spoon 1/2 teaspoon of the goat cheese into the center of the date where the pit once lived, and then close up the date. Wrap the date with one bacon strip, spiraling to cover the whole date, and secure it in place with a toothpick. Place the date on a baking sheet and repeat for remaining dates, cheese, and bacon strips. Bake in the oven for approximately 15-20 minutes, flipping the toothpick half-way through. Remove from heat, let rest for 5 minutes, then serve.

CHICKEN QUESO DIP

(Yield 3.5 cups)

2 cups rotisserie chicken, shredded
1 8-ounce brick of cream cheese
1/2 cup Greek yogurt
1 4-ounce can of diced fire roasted green chiles
1/2 – 1 tablespoon chipotle peppers in adobo sauce—finely chopped

Combine all ingredients in a Le Creuset pot or slow cooker on low heat. Cover and cook for 30 minutes, stirring occasionally to combine ingredients.

Serve with Almond Flour Pita Chips (see p.10).

Mango Salsa

(Yield 1.5 cups)

Mango salsa has a little sweet and a little spicy going on, which makes it the perfect accompaniment to a cheese plate, a dip for veggies, or a topping on grilled chicken or fish. I like to eat it straight from the bowl with just a fork, but maybe that's just me.

1 mango, peeled and chopped
2-3 tomatoes, tops cut off and discarded, chopped
1/2 jalapeño pepper, chopped
Juice of 1 lime
1/4 cup cilantro leaves
1/4 onion, minced

For a chunky salsa, hand chop all ingredients and mix together.

For a smooth salsa, loosely chop all ingredients, then pulse in blender or food processor until desired thickness.

Roasted Red Pepper Hummus

(Yield 2 cups)

2 15-ounce cans organic garbanzo beans, rinsed and drained
1/2 cup tahini
1 teaspoon minced garlic (about 2 cloves)
1/2 of a 12-ounce jar of roasted red peppers in water,
plus 2 tablespoons of the water
1 teaspoon chili powder
1 teaspoon salt
1/2 teaspoon cumin
Juice of 1/2 lemon
2 tablespoons olive oil

Place all ingredients except the olive oil in Vitamix® or similar blender/food processor, blend on medium high, mashing down the ingredients with the masher wand, for about 1-2 minutes. Stop blending, remove lid, and scrape down sides. Replace lid and continue blending another 1-2 minutes while drizzling oil slowly into hummus. Check that texture of hummus is desired consistency, if not, continue blending until smooth, being careful not to over blend. Serve with veggies and Almond Flour Pita Chips (see p.10).

Cheese Ball

(Yield 1 cheese ball. It's a ball. Made from cheese.)

1 8-ounce brick of cream cheese, softened to room temperature
1 cup of shredded cheddar cheese, finely chopped
1/2 cup freshly grated parmesan
1/2 small brown or yellow onion, finely minced
1 teaspoon Worcestershire sauce
1 teaspoon Dijon mustard
1/8 teaspoon cayenne
1/2 cup slivered almonds

In a large mixing bowl, mash up the cream cheese, cheddar, parmesan, onion, Worcestershire sauce, Dijon mustard and cayenne with a flat spatula. Keep mashing and within a few minutes it will be soft enough to mix ingredients evenly.

Form mixture into a ball, sculpting until it becomes an even round shape with a flat bottom. Wrap in plastic wrap and let harden in the fridge, about 3-5 hours.

Meanwhile, pour slivered almonds onto a flat plate. Using the bottom side of a sturdy glass or ramekin, crush the slivered almonds into smaller pieces. Heat a non-stick sauté pan to medium high heat and toast almond pieces, tossing and stirring consistently so that the smaller almond pieces don't burn. Remove from heat when golden brown with a few white flecks of almond slivers left. Set on plate to let cool.

When cheese ball is firm, remove from fridge and roll exterior onto the toasted almond slivers to coat. Serve immediately with Almond Flour Pita Chips (see p.10), or refrigerate until ready to serve.

Chapter Two: Mains

Cauliflower Pizza Crust

(Yields 1 10" thin crust)

2 12-ounce bags of cauliflower florets, stems removed
1/4 cup grated parmesan
1/4 cup shredded mozzarella
1/2 teaspoon garlic powder
1/2 teaspoon dried oregano
1/2 teaspoon dried basil
1/2 teaspoon salt
1 egg

For topping:
Homemade Pizza Sauce (see p. 173), or store bought without sugar
Your choice of meat, veg, cheese, etc.

Pulse cauliflower in a food processor until it resembles the texture of couscous. It will have a snowy appearance.

In a microwave safe bowl, cook on high for 3-4 minutes. Let cool. Using cheesecloth, squeeze any and all excess water out of the cauliflower, then do one final squeeze wrapping a towel around the cheesecloth to make sure all excess water has been removed.

Preheat oven to 425°. In a large mixing bowl, mix cauliflower, parmesan, mozzarella, garlic powder, oregano, basil, salt, and egg very evenly and form a dough ball.

Cover a baking sheet with parchment paper. Spray it with a light coating of olive oil or coconut oil. Place dough ball in center, and press into a circle, about 10-11 inches in diameter and 1/2 inch thick.

Bake in oven for 11-14 minutes until golden brown spots start to cover the surface of the crust. Remove from oven, add your sauce and toppings, and place back in oven for 5-7 minutes or until cheese topping is melted and bubbly.

Ultimate Low Carb Pizza Crust

(Yields 1 10-12 inch thin crust pizza)

Recipes are fluid … always evolving, always improving. And in my case, I'm always improvising based on what I have available in the kitchen. I love it when you guys find a new way—a better way—to make my recipes, and then tweet me a picture. It means that we're having a conversation, and there's nothing that food does better than invoke wonderful conversation.

This low carb pizza crust is an adaptation of the pizza crust recipe posted on the site for the documentary film "Fat Head". I have tinkered with this crust to get it where I want it-just a tad more chewy and moist, with added dried herbs for some solid Italian flavor components. Hope y'all enjoy. And be sure to tweet me a pic when you change it up and make it your own.

For crust:

1 1/2 cups grated mozzarella (fresh is bestest)	2/3 cup almond flour
3 tablespoons cream cheese	1/2 teaspoon dried oregano
1 egg	1/2 teaspoon dried basil
	1/2 teaspoon garlic salt

For topping:

Homemade Pizza Sauce (see p. 173), or store bought without sugar
Your choice of meat, veg, cheese, etc.
In the above pic, I pre-cooked hot Italian sausage, grated mozzarella and fontina cheeses, and topped with arugula when fresh out of the oven.

Preheat oven to 425°. Microwave the mozzarella and cream cheese in a large bowl until soft and pliable, about 30 seconds. Add egg, almond flour, oregano, and basil. Blend well into a dough ball. Press into a circle or square shape on a parchment-lined baking sheet. Sprinkle garlic salt over surface of pizza crust. Pierce surface with fork to prevent rising of the crust while baking.

Bake crust in oven for 8-10 minutes. Pierce again with fork if bubbles form. Bake another 2-4 minutes if crust has not already browned. Do not over bake as it will dry out!

Add pizza sauce and toppings, pop back in the oven for 4-5 more minutes until cheese is melted and bubbly.

SESAME CRUSTED SEARED AHI

(Serves 2-4)

1 pound of sashimi grade ahi tuna steaks
1 tablespoon gluten-free soy sauce
1 teaspoon wasabi paste (optional)
1/2 teaspoon fresh pepper
1/4 cup black or white sesame seeds or a combination of both
1 tablespoon olive oil

Dredge tuna steaks in soy sauce, rub wasabi paste into steaks if desired, season with black pepper.

Lay the sesame seeds on a flat plate. Press the tuna steaks into the sesame seeds to encrust the outside of the steaks.

Heat olive oil in a non-stick pan to medium high heat. Sear the tuna steaks, about 3-4 minutes on each side, keeping the tuna raw in the middle but seared on the outside edges. With a very sharp knife, slice tuna into strips. Serve with additional gluten-free soy sauce for dipping, if desired.

Pistachio Crusted Coriander Salmon

(Serves 2-4)

1 cup shelled pistachios
1/8 teaspoon celery salt
1/4 teaspoon cardamom
1/4 teaspoon coriander
1/2 teaspoon onion powder
1/4 teaspoon fresh cracked
  pepper

2 tablespoons of olive oil
  (plus more to coat pan)
Salt
2-4 wild-caught salmon fillets
Lemon wedges for garnish

Preheat oven to 350°. Grind up pistachios in food processor or Vitamix® so that there is still some variance in the texture of the nuts (some of it should be finely ground, and a little should be more coarsely ground). Remove ground pistachios from blender and put in bowl. Add celery salt, cardamom, coriander, onion powder, fresh cracked pepper, 2 tablespoons of olive oil and mix together into a paste. Salt salmon fillets and then coat them with the pistachio mixture. Place fillets in an oiled cast iron skillet or baking pan skin side down. Bake in oven for 30 minutes, checking on it every 10 minutes. If you notice it starting to burn on top (pistachios are very delicate), cover the pan with aluminum foil for the remainder of the cooking time. Remove from oven, garnish with lemon and enjoy!

SALMON WITH LEMON DIJON BASIL SAUCE

(Serves 3-4)

This brightly colored salmon dish is always a crowd pleaser. It's an easy go-to salmon recipe in my house that you can whip up in less than 25 minutes if you are into speed cooking. If you use wild-caught sockeye salmon, the cooking time generally is shorter, so make sure you check the salmon after 15 minutes of cooking. The darker pink color is deceiving, and it has a tendency to stay dark pink even when cooked all the way through.

1-2 pounds wild caught salmon fillets
Salt and pepper
1/4 cup olive oil plus more for oiling the salmon skin
1/4 cup lemon juice
1 teaspoon minced lemon zest
2 tablespoons Dijon mustard
7-8 basil leaves, chopped
1 clove minced garlic

Light grill or preheat oven to 400°.

Clean salmon, making sure any stray scales or pin bones are removed. Oil the skin. Lay on foil-lined baking sheet, pink side up. Season lightly with salt and pepper.

In a food processor or Vitamix®, pulse olive oil, lemon juice, zest, mustard, basil leaves, and garlic. Pour evenly over salmon so it's coated thickly.

Grill, skin side down, about 15 minutes, until desired doneness. Or bake in oven at 400° for about 15 minutes until desired doneness.

Almond Crusted Baked Cod

(Serves 2-4)

4 tablespoons of butter
1 shallot, minced
1 teaspoon garlic, minced
1 teaspoon of chives, minced
1 cup almond flour
2 tablespoons mayonnaise
1 egg yolk
1 teaspoon lemon zest, minced
1 pound cod fillets
Salt and pepper for seasoning

Preheat oven to 325°.

In a sauté pan, melt the butter to medium high heat until bubbling. Sauté the shallots until they start to brown, about 3 minutes. Add garlic and chives and cook another minute. Pour in almond flour. Stir and cook for 3-4 minutes. Remove from heat, transfer to a shallow dish, and let cool.

In a small bowl, whisk together mayonnaise, egg yolk, and lemon zest. Pat the cod fillets well with a paper towel to ensure they are dry. Season fish with salt and pepper. Using a pastry brush, brush the mayonnaise mixture onto your cod fillets.

Press the fillets into the almond flour mixture, evenly breading them. Place fillets onto an oiled wire rack, which has been placed over a baking sheet.

Bake for 20-25 minutes, or until fillets are cooked through.

Asian Marinated Shrimp Skewers

(Serves 4-6)

1-2 lbs. peeled, deveined shrimp
1/3 cup olive oil
Splash of sesame oil
1 tablespoon grated fresh ginger
1 tablespoon fish sauce
1 garlic clove, minced
1 tablespoon gluten-free soy sauce
1/2 teaspoon chili garlic sauce (look for the jar with the rooster on it)
2 stalks of fresh lemongrass diced, or 1 tablespoon of lemongrass in a tube

---

Rinse and pat dry shrimp, then put shrimp into a large plastic baggie. Whisk together remaining ingredients and pour marinade over shrimp in the plastic baggie. Seal baggie and marinate for 30 minutes to 1 hour. Soak 8-10 bamboo skewers in water for 10 minutes, then remove from water and pat dry excess water. Skewer 4-6 shrimp per bamboo skewer.

Preheat grill to 450°, grill shrimp 2-3 minutes per side, or until they turn from translucent to opaque.

Coconut Crusted Shrimp

(Serves 2-4)

To make this recipe dairy free, you can replace the yogurt and milk with one cup of coconut milk.

---

1 cup unsweetened coconut flakes
1/2 cup full fat plain yogurt
1 egg
1/4 cup milk
1 teaspoon grated ginger
1 pound deveined, peeled shrimp, fresh or thawed from frozen
Salt and pepper
1/2 cup coconut oil

Preheat oven to 350°. Spread coconut flakes evenly on a baking sheet, toast in oven 5-6 minutes, tossing flakes once to avoid burning. Remove from oven, let cool, and pour into a shallow bowl.

In another shallow bowl, whisk together yogurt, egg, milk, and grated ginger. Dab shrimp with a paper towel to ensure that all are dry, and then season with salt and pepper.

In an iron skillet, heat coconut oil to high heat. While oil heats, one by one, dredge the shrimp in the liquid mixture, then roll in the coconut flakes until coated.

Test your oil by dropping a few coconut flakes in the iron skillet. If they sizzle, the oil is hot enough to start cooking the shrimp.

Sauté the shrimp on high heat, 2 minutes on each side. Coconut crust will become golden but not charred. Remove from oil carefully and place on paper towels to drain excess oil. Serve immediately with Mango Salsa (see p. 23).

CHILI LIME FLAT IRON STEAK

(Serves 4-6)

1 tablespoon chili powder
1/2 teaspoon Ancho Chile powder
2 teaspoons salt
1/2 teaspoon pepper
1 tablespoon olive oil
1-3 pound flat iron steak
Juice of 1 lime
Cilantro, chopped for garnish

Mix together chili powder, Ancho Chile powder, salt, pepper, and olive oil and rub into steak. Marinate in fridge for 1-4 hours.

Heat grill to 500°, then grill flat iron steak 5-7 minutes per side, until desired doneness. Squeeze juice of one lime over the steak upon removal from grill. Slice and serve immediately. Garnish with cilantro.

Leek and Mustard Crusted Tenderloin

(Serves 4-6)

2-3 pound beef tenderloin
Salt & pepper
2 tablespoons olive oil
1 tablespoon spicy brown mustard
1/2 teaspoon minced garlic
2 leeks, white and palest green part only, chopped
1/2 cup freshly grated parmesan
1/2 cup almond flour

Preheat oven to 425°. Bring beef tenderloin to room temperature. Generously season beef with salt and pepper. Roast on a foil covered pan for 20 minutes.

In a food processor or Vitamix®, combine olive oil, mustard, garlic, leeks, and parmesan until it becomes a thick paste, scraping down the sides. In a medium bowl, add the leek paste to the almond flour, mixing well.

Remove the beef from the oven and evenly coat it with the leek almond flour paste, being careful not to burn your hands. Place coated beef back into oven. Continue to roast for an additional 20-25 minutes until crust is golden brown. Remove from oven, let stand for 15 minutes, then slice and serve.

Southwest Style Burgers

(Yield 4 burgers)

---

1 pound of 80/20 ground beef
1/2 tablespoon of chipotle peppers in adobo sauce, minced
1 4-ounce can of fire-roasted diced green chiles, drained
1 teaspoon of Ancho Chile powder
1 teaspoon of salt
3-4 ounces Monterey Jack cheese
1/2 avocado, sliced

Throw the beef, peppers, minced chipotle peppers, diced green chiles, Chile powder, and salt into a bowl and mix together with your hands. Form into 4-5 patties making an indentation with your thumb in the middle of the patty.

Cook on medium high heat in a cast iron skillet, or throw on the grill, cooking 5-6 minutes per side or until cooked through. Melt cheese onto burger patty, serve with avocado slices.

PAN FRIED BONE-IN RIB EYE

(Serves 1-2)

This pan steak is so delicious I can barely keep them around long enough to photograph them. It's the most foolproof steak I've ever made, but everyone who eats it thinks it's fancy. This means you can celebrate with a juicy rib eye pretty much anytime, without having to pay steakhouse prices. I use a 10-inch cast iron skillet, but any flat sauté pan will do.

8-10 ounce bone-in rib eye steak
1/2 teaspoon truffle salt
1/2 teaspoon sea salt
1/4 teaspoon freshly ground pepper
1 teaspoon balsamic vinegar
1/2 tablespoon butter

Remove steak from fridge. Season one side of steak by rubbing truffle salt into steak. Season other side by rubbing salt, pepper, and the balsamic vinegar into steak. Let stand 15 minutes.

Heat butter on medium high heat in a heavy cast iron skillet until bubbling, almost browning. Place steak into pan, balsamic side down, cooking 6 minutes per side for a medium rare steak. Press steak in the middle to judge desired doneness. Remove steak from heat, let stand for 5-10 minutes before serving.

SKIRT STEAK SKEWERS

(Serves 2-4)

---

1 pound of skirt steak (also called flap meat)
Salt & pepper
5-6 skewers

Bring steak to room temperature for 20-30 minutes before cooking. If you are using wooden or bamboo skewers, make sure that you soak the skewers in water while you are bringing the steak to room temperature. Cut the steak into thin slices, about 1 1/2" wide, and arrange on the skewers. Salt and pepper the meat. Preheat cast iron pan to very high heat before you place the meat on it. Once hot, add the meat and cook 4-5 minutes per side for medium doneness, longer if you prefer it well done. Serve with a side of Chimichurri Sauce (see p. 179).

GREEK FLANK STEAK

(Serves 2-4)

1 tablespoon fresh oregano, minced
1 teaspoon fresh mint, minced
1 teaspoon lemon zest, minced
Juice of 1 lemon
1/2 cup olive oil
1/2 teaspoon garlic powder
1 teaspoon salt
1/2 teaspoon pepper
1 pound flank steak

Combine oregano, mint, lemon zest, lemon juice, olive oil, garlic powder, salt, and pepper. Pour over flank steak, coating all sides, and marinate for 30 minutes to 2 hours.

Oven Instructions:

Preheat oven to 450°. Remove flank steak from marinade, discarding marinade. Heat a sauté pan to high heat. Sear flank steak 3 minutes on each side, until you get a nice brown sear. Move flank steak to a roasting pan. Finish flank steak in oven 15-18 minutes to medium doneness. Remove from oven, let rest for 5 minutes. Slice into diagonal strips. Serve with grilled veggies or on a salad with a side of tzatziki sauce.

Grill Instructions:

Heat grill to 500-550°. Grill flank steak, 7-9 minutes per side for medium doneness. Let rest for 5 minutes. Slice on the diagonal and serve.

Machaca

(Serves 6-8)

This recipe is brought to you by my friend, Joann Neil, where it was highlighted on her blog www.dailycupofjo.com. For the past ten years, Joann has been teaching me her wise ways, including how to be a better writer and how to multitask with three kids (seriously, this lady is superwoman). She was my original running mentor, having completed myriad marathons before I ever put on a pair of running shoes. Plus, she always praises me for using "myriad" properly, so hopefully she'll read this and send me a text. She was the first one to encourage me to start running and gave me permission to call myself a runner even though I never aspired to do more than a 5K. All of her recipes are fantastic, but this here machaca smells so good, everyone in the house will flip out, which is always the goal.

---

3 1/2 – 4 pounds beef loin tri-tip roast or brisket
1/3 cup ground coffee
3 tablespoons Ancho Chile powder
1/4 cup salt
2 tablespoons olive oil
1 1/2 cups red wine
1 3/4 cups tomato juice
3 tablespoons fresh lime juice

3/4 cup red wine vinegar
6 cloves garlic, chopped
1 tablespoon fresh ground black pepper
2 teaspoons cinnamon
2 bay leaves
1/2 brown onion, chopped
1/2 red onion, chopped
Avocado slices and sour cream, for serving

Cut the meat into five large pieces. Whisk together coffee, Ancho Chile powder, and salt in a bowl and season the meat pieces with the mixture, pressing it in. Heat the olive oil in a large skillet on medium-high, and brown the meat to caramelize the surface. Remove from heat, let cool slightly, and cut into 2-inch cubes.

Transfer the meat to a Dutch oven or slow cooker. Cover with the wine, tomato, and lime juices, vinegar, garlic, pepper, cinnamon, bay leaves, and chopped onion. Cover with a lid or foil and braise on low heat for 3 to 4 hours. If using a slow cooker, cook on high 3-4 hours.

Use a slotted spoon to transfer the meat to a surface where you can shred it. Serve it at once with avocado and sour cream.

Sirloin Steak and Spinach Salad

(Serves 2-4)

1 1/2 pounds sirloin steak
1 tablespoon olive oil
1 teaspoon balsamic vinegar
1 teaspoon Worcestershire sauce
1/2 cup pecan pieces
1/2 cup buttermilk
1/4 cup mayonnaise
2 teaspoons apple cider vinegar
Dash of salt & pepper
4 cups fresh spinach
1 pear, thinly sliced
1 cup grape or cherry tomatoes, halved

Dredge the sirloin steak in a mixture of the olive oil, balsamic vinegar, and Worcestershire sauce. Let stand for 30 minutes, or up to 8 hours in the fridge. Bring back to room temperature while heating up your grill to 450°. Grill the sirloin steak, about 8-10 minutes each side for medium doneness. If you want to pan fry your steak, heat up a cast iron pan on high heat, and cook the steak 8-10 minutes per side or until desired doneness. Remove steak from heat and let rest for 10-15 minutes.

While steak is cooking, preheat oven to 350°. Place the pecan pieces onto a baking sheet and lightly toast in oven for 5-8 minutes, being careful not to burn. In a bowl, whisk together buttermilk, mayonnaise, apple cider vinegar, and a dash of salt and pepper into your dressing.

In a large salad bowl, toss spinach, pear slices, cherry tomatoes, and pecan pieces. Cut sirloin steak into 1/4-inch slices, and toss into salad. Dress with the buttermilk dressing.

Shepherd's Pie with Cauliflower Mash

(Serves 4-6)

2 cups of fresh cremini
   mushrooms, chopped
2 tablespoons olive oil
1 finely chopped brown, yellow,
   or Vidalia onion
6-8 baby carrots, shredded
1-2 garlic cloves, minced
1 tablespoon fresh parsley, chopped
1/4 teaspoon onion salt
1/4 teaspoon garlic salt
1/4 teaspoon dried thyme
1/4 teaspoon dried oregano

1 pound ground beef
1 pound ground pork
1 teaspoon chicken bouillon paste
   or a cube of chicken bouillon,
   smashed into powder
Salt and pepper to taste
1 head of cauliflower cut into chunks
1/4 cup cream cheese
1/4 cup heavy cream
Salt for seasoning
1/2 cup grated fresh parmesan

On medium high heat, sauté mushrooms in 1 tablespoon of olive oil, until nicely browned. Set aside.

Sauté onion in 1 tablespoon of olive oil until soft, about 8 minutes. Add in carrot, garlic, parsley, onion salt, garlic salt, thyme, and oregano, and sauté another 5-10 minutes until soft. Set aside with mushrooms.

Sauté ground beef and pork, stirring meat until it is minced and cooked through. Drain and put back into the pan. Add in the chicken bouillon and mix evenly. Add in mushrooms and onion mixture and mix evenly. Season with salt and pepper to taste if necessary.

Preheat oven to 350°. Meanwhile, boil the cauliflower in a large pot of water for 8-11 minutes, until tender when pierced with a fork. Drain well, press as dry as possible with paper towels. In a blender or food processor, place cauliflower, cream cheese, and heavy cream. Process into the consistency of mashed potatoes, seasoning with salt halfway through, and adding more liquid if necessary.

Transfer the meat mixture into a deep casserole dish. Spread cauliflower mash over the meat and top with thin coat of freshly grated parmesan.

Bake for 30-40 minutes, or until parmesan is lightly golden on top.

ZUCCHINI PASTA BOLOGNESE

(Serves 2-4)

Oh, how I love thee, Paderno Spiralizer! This contraption has single-handedly replaced my beloved pasta with much healthier zucchini noodles. I don't mean to pressure you or anything, but if you don't have a spiralizer, you NEED to get one. Now. Go ahead. I'll wait.

---

4 tablespoons olive oil, divided
1 medium onion, finely diced
1 medium carrot, or 6 baby carrots,
  finely diced
1 celery stalk, finely diced
2 ounces thickly sliced pancetta
1 pound ground beef
2 large garlic cloves, chopped, or
  1 teaspoon of minced garlic
1 teaspoon butter
2 teaspoons salt
1/2 teaspoon pepper

1/2 teaspoon garlic powder
1/2 teaspoon onion powder
1 28-ounce can peeled Italian tomatoes
  —seeded and finely chopped,
  juices reserved
1/2 cup chicken broth
1/2 teaspoon dried thyme
1 bay leaf
Salt and pepper
1/4 cup half & half
2 pounds spiralized zucchini pasta
Freshly grated parmesan, for serving

Heat 1 tablespoon of the olive oil in a large, heavy saucepan until shimmering. Add the onion, carrot, celery, and pancetta and cook over moderate heat, stirring occasionally, until the vegetables are softened but not browned, about 8 minutes. Scrape the vegetable mixture into a large bowl.

Add the remaining 3 tablespoons of olive oil to the saucepan and heat until just shimmering.

Add the ground meat and cook over moderately high heat until just barely pink, about 5 minutes. Return the vegetable mixture to the saucepan. Add the garlic, butter, salt, pepper, garlic powder, and onion powder, and cook over high heat until fragrant, about 1 minute.

Stir in the tomatoes and their juices, the chicken broth, thyme, and bay leaf. Season with a generous pinch of salt and pepper and bring to a boil over high heat. Cover partially and cook over medium low heat for 30 minutes. Discard the bay leaf. Stir in the half and half until well blended.

Add your spiralized zucchini pasta to the sauce, tossing evenly. Cover and simmer an additional 30 minutes, or until pasta is desired firmness. Season with additional salt and pepper once or twice. Serve pasta with freshly grated parmesan.

PORK CHOP DRY RUB

(Serves 2-3)

1 teaspoon salt
1 teaspoon fresh pepper
1 teaspoon garlic powder
1 teaspoon onion powder
1 teaspoon gluten-free soy sauce
1 teaspoon smoked paprika
1 teaspoon olive oil, plus additional for baking sheet if cooking in oven
1 teaspoon ground espresso (optional, but adds a delicious flavor)
1 pound of bone-in pork chops (about 2-3)

Combine all the ingredients together until it becomes a gritty paste. Rub all over the meaty part of your pork chops. Let stand room temp for 15-20 minutes before grilling/cooking.

Grill Instructions:

Heat up grill to 500°, cook pork chops 5-7 minutes per side.

Oven Instructions:

Heat oven to 450°. Line baking sheet with foil. Spread a thin layer of olive oil only where the pork chops will be placed. Place pork chops on baking sheet, bake in oven 18-20 minutes, flipping chops halfway through.

Pork Tenderloin Medallions

(Serves 2-4)

1.5-2.5 pounds pork tenderloin, trimmed of excess fat

Marinade:
1/3 cup olive oil
1/4 cup gluten-free soy sauce
1/8 cup orange juice
1 tablespoon Dijon mustard
1 garlic clove, minced
1/2 teaspoon fresh ground pepper
Dash of cayenne

Whisk together marinade ingredients. Pour into a large plastic baggie.

Drop pork tenderloin into bag of marinade, sealing it well and swishing the marinade around the tenderloin. Marinate in the fridge 1-8 hours, until you are ready to start cooking.

Grill Instructions:

Prepare/heat grill up to 500-550°. Remove tenderloin from marinade (discarding excess marinade) and grill for 15-20 minutes until desired doneness. Let stand for 5-10 minutes, then slice and serve. Pork tenderloin can have a slight pale pink hue in the middle (not raw, mind you, just slightly pink), and it will still cook while standing.

Oven Instructions:

Preheat oven to 425°. Remove tenderloin from marinade, wrap tenderloin in aluminum foil. Cook in oven for 25-30 minutes until desired doneness. Let stand for 5-10 minutes after removing from oven, then slice and serve. Pork tenderloin can have a slight pale pink hue in the middle (not raw, mind you, just slightly pink), and it will still cook while standing, steaming itself in the aluminum foil. You can also use the juices in the aluminum foil to drizzle on the pork when you slice and serve, if you are so inspired (I usually am).

FLAMENQUINES

(Serves 4)

Who wants to roll up some pork in another kind of pork, bread it, fry it, and eat it? I do. And I did.

---

1 pound of 1/2-inch thick boneless pork loin chops (about 5 pork chops)
Salt
Freshly ground pepper
Thin slices of prosciutto ham
2 eggs
1 tablespoon whole milk
1 1/4 cups almond flour
Olive oil for frying
Mayonnaise for serving

Trim excess loose fat from pork chops. Working with 1 pork chop at a time, place between 2 sheets of plastic wrap and pound into a 1/4-inch thick cutlet. Arrange the cutlets on a work surface and season with salt on one side, and pepper lightly on both sides. Cover each cutlet with a slice of prosciutto and roll lengthwise into a cylinder.

In a shallow bowl, beat the eggs with the milk. Dip the pork rolls in the egg mixture, then in the almond flour, pressing on them lightly. Transfer to a plate until ready to cook.

In a cast iron skillet, heat 1/4-inch of olive oil until shimmering. Test the heat of the oil by dropping a few bits of almond flour into the pan. If it fries up quickly without burning, you are ready to go. Add the pork rolls and fry over moderate heat, rotating every few minutes, until an instant-read thermometer inserted in the center registers 155°, about 5–8 minutes. Transfer the rolls to paper towels, cut once in the center on the diagonal. Serve hot, with a dollop of mayonnaise on the side.

Orange Ginger Pork Chops

(Serves 4)

1 teaspoon orange zest
Juice of 1/2 of the orange
1 tablespoon olive oil
2 tablespoons gluten-free soy sauce
1 teaspoon minced garlic
1 tablespoon fresh ginger, cut into chunks
1/2 teaspoon garlic chili paste
Salt & pepper
4 bone-in pork chops

Place orange zest, juice of half the orange, olive oil, soy sauce, minced garlic, ginger chunks, and chili paste into Vitamix®, blender, or food processor. Pulse for 10-15 seconds until marinade is smooth.

Salt and pepper the pork chops, place in a plastic baggie and pour in marinade. Seal and refrigerate chops, letting them marinate for 30 minutes to 8 hours.

Heat up a grill to 500°, or bring a cast iron skillet to medium high heat. Cook pork chops 6-8 minutes per side, or until cooked through.

PORK SCALOPPINI

(Serves 4–5)

---

2 tablespoons olive oil
1 teaspoon rosemary, finely chopped
1 teaspoon capers, chopped
1 teaspoon minced garlic
Juice of one lemon
Salt and pepper for seasoning
1 pound boneless pork chops, pounded to 1/2-inch thickness
1 tablespoon butter

Combine the olive oil, rosemary, capers, garlic, lemon juice, salt, and pepper in a shallow pan or bowl. Place the pork chops in there and marinate in the fridge, preferably for at least an hour.

Preheat a grill to 500°, or heat up butter in a cast iron skillet on high heat. Grill or sauté the pork chops for 4–5 minutes per side.

Boneless Country Style Pork Ribs

(Serves 6-8)

1 1/2 teaspoons onion powder
1 teaspoon smoked paprika
1 teaspoon salt (plus additional for seasoning)
1/2 teaspoon pepper (plus additional for seasoning)
2 pounds boneless pork loin country style ribs
1/4 cup olive oil
1 onion thinly sliced
1 teaspoon minced garlic
1/2 teaspoon minced fresh thyme
1 cup chicken broth
1 tablespoon apple cider vinegar

Combine onion powder, smoked paprika, salt, and pepper in a small bowl. Pat dry pork with paper towels, and then season with the spice mixture. Heat 1/8 cup of the olive oil in a pan. Once heated, add the pork and cook until it is well browned, about 4 minutes per side. Remove from the pan and set aside on a plate.

Add remaining olive oil and onion to the skillet. Cover and cook until the onions are soft and golden brown, about 5-7 minutes. Then add the garlic and thyme for an additional minute. Add broth and bring to a boil. Return the pork to the pan, cover, and reduce the heat to low. Cook until tender, about 15 minutes. Transfer pork to a plate. Stir vinegar into the sauce and spoon over pork.

ASIAN PORK LOIN ROAST

(Serves 4–8)

3–4 pound pork loin roast
Salt and pepper for seasoning
3 tablespoons olive oil, divided
1 sweet onion, sliced
2 garlic cloves, minced
1 lime, juiced
3 tablespoons gluten-free soy sauce
1 teaspoon dried mustard
1 teaspoon fresh pepper
1-inch chunk of fresh peeled ginger
1/2 teaspoon of Chinese Five Spice powder
1 teaspoon fish sauce
1 teaspoon lemon grass paste
1/2 teaspoon garlic chili paste
3 tablespoons water

Season the pork loin roast with salt and pepper. Heat 1 tablespoon of the olive oil in a sauté pan on medium high heat. Sear the roast, browning all sides, about 2–3 minutes per side. Remove from heat and place in a slow cooker.

Place onions in slow cooker surrounding and covering roast.

In a medium bowl, whisk remaining ingredients together into a marinade. Pour entire bowl of marinade over roast. Cover and cook on high in slow cooker for 4–6 hours.

Fast(er) Carnitas

(Serves 8-10)

2 teaspoons salt
1 teaspoon pepper
2 teaspoons oregano
1 teaspoon cumin
2 tablespoons olive oil
2-4 pound pork butt or shoulder roast
5 garlic cloves, minced
1 onion, loosely chopped
1 orange, sliced in half
Dusting of cinnamon
Queso fresco, fresh cilantro, and lime wedges for serving (optional)

Mix salt, pepper, oregano, cumin, and olive oil into a paste. Rub into pork. Place in slow cooker, top with garlic and onion. Squeeze orange halves over pork, drop halves into the slow cooker. Dust with cinnamon, cover, and cook on high for 4 hours.

Preheat oven to 300°.

Pull apart pork with fork, remove and discard larger pieces of fat. Spread pork in roasting pan, pour liquid and onions from the slow cooker over the meat. Heat in oven for 20 minutes or until pork is crispy on the ends. Serve hot with queso fresco, fresh cilantro, and lime wedges.

Herb Roasted Lamb Chops

(Serves 4-6)

2 pounds lamb loin chops
Salt and pepper
1 tablespoon minced fresh rosemary
4 garlic cloves, minced
1 teaspoon fresh thyme leaves
1/2 teaspoon dried oregano
2 tablespoons olive oil

Preheat oven to 400°.

Place chops in a foil-lined baking dish. Generously salt and pepper both sides of each chop. Combine rosemary, garlic, thyme, oregano, and olive oil in a bowl to make a paste. Rub each side of each chop with the paste.

Heat up a sauté pan. Once heated, add chops and brown 2 minutes per side. Return chops to the foil-lined baking dish, scraping any remnants of herbs from the sauté pan. Bake in oven 20-25 minutes depending on how rare you would like them.

Easiest Roasted Chicken Ever

(Serves 2-4)

When you learn how to roast the perfect chicken, you will always be able to feed the people on relatively few ingredients. Roast chicken warms up your house, and makes it smell oh so good. Pro tip: Cook the chicken in a smaller pan, and the juices will drip down and caramelize the onions. Serve those caramelized bad boys alongside the chicken, and you'll look like a hero.

1 organic free range young chicken (3-4 pounds)
1/4 cup sea salt
1 onion, sliced thinly
2 tablespoons of butter, cut into smaller pieces
3 lemon slices
Herbs (whatever is on hand: basil, parsley, sage, rosemary, and/or thyme)
2 tablespoons olive oil
Pepper for seasoning
1/4 cup chicken broth (optional if needed to start the basting juices)

Wash out the chicken, pat dry with paper towels. Remove all giblets if there are any. Rub half of sea salt all over chicken. Pour remaining salt into the chicken cavity. Set chicken on plate in fridge for 30 minutes to 4 hours.

Pull chicken out of fridge, let stand for 20 minutes. Preheat oven to 400°.

In a square 8 x 8 glass baking pan, place the onion slices on their sides covering the bottom of the pan in a single layer. Place the chicken, breast side up, directly atop the onions.

Using your index finger, separate the chicken skin from the breast. Shove little pieces of the butter, two on each side, under the skin and pull skin back over the breasts. Place lemon slices into cavity of chicken, then stuff the herbs into the cavity, slightly sticking out. Finally, rub the olive oil evenly all over the chicken, season with pepper.

Place in oven and bake for 15 minutes, then baste. Turn oven down to 375°, and continue roasting 1 more hour, basting every 15 minutes. If your oven is dry, you can pour chicken broth under the chicken over the onions to get basting juices going. If your heat is very strong and looking like it might burn the breast skin, put a piece of aluminum foil over the chicken. The chicken is done when you slice into the crevice between the leg and breast and the juices run clear.

ALMOND CRUSTED CHICKEN BREAST MILANESE

(Serves 4)

Chicken Milanese is a fancy way of saying "fried chicken cutlet." This dish stands on its own as an easy weeknight dinner. You can cut the chicken into strips and you'll have chicken fingers for the kiddies, or you can fancy it up by taking a few extra steps and turn it into a Chicken Parm.

---

4 chicken breasts, pounded to 1/2-inch thickness
Salt & Pepper
1 cup almond flour (same as almond *meal* flour)
2 tablespoons olive oil

Salt and pepper your chicken breasts well. Pour the almond flour into a shallow bowl. Press the chicken into the flour, coating the breast entirely.

Heat 1 tablespoon of the oil in a non-stick pan on medium high heat, making sure the oil shimmers before putting the chicken in the pan. Cook 2 breasts, about 5-8 minutes on each side, until cooked through and the almond flour has turned a nice brown color. Add the second tablespoon of oil. Let it get hot, and then add the second two chicken breasts, cooking each side 5-8 minutes until cooked through.

CHICKEN PARM

(Serves 3-4)

Marinara
2 tablespoons of olive oil
1 teaspoon minced garlic
7-10 basil leaves, chopped
2 14-ounce cans of tomatoes, puréed
1/2 can tomato paste (3 ounces)
1 teaspoon salt, plus more for seasoning
Pepper
1 tablespoon butter

Chicken
1 pound boneless chicken breasts, trimmed and pounded to a 1/2-inch thickness
Salt and pepper
1 cup almond flour for breading
2 tablespoons olive oil
1 cup shredded mozzarella

Preheat oven to 350°. In a medium saucepan, heat olive oil to medium high heat and sauté garlic and basil for 2-3 minutes. Add in puréed tomatoes, tomato paste, 1 teaspoon of salt, and a twist of fresh pepper. Bring the tomatoes to a boil, and add the butter while stirring with a wooden spoon. Turn the heat down to low. Let the sauce simmer while prepping the chicken, seasoning with a little extra salt and pepper every 10 minutes.

Season chicken breasts with salt and pepper. In a shallow bowl, spread out almond flour. Dredge the chicken breasts in the almond flour to coat. Heat olive oil on medium high heat in a sauté pan until it shimmers from being very hot, but being careful not to let the oil start smoking. Cook the coated chicken breasts for 6-7 minutes per side. Transfer chicken to a casserole pan.

Sprinkle half of the mozzarella on the chicken breasts. Ladle sauce over the chicken/mozzarella, covering completely (reserve some sauce for serving). Sprinkle remaining mozzarella cheese over sauce and chicken. Bake in oven for 10 minutes, or until cheese is melted and bubbly. Serve with additional reserved sauce, if desired.

Torri's "Fried" Chicken Legs

(Serves 4-6)

How did Torri's "Fried" Chicken Legs cross the road? Very carefully ... on a surface made of non-stick foil.

Torri Anders has been my trainer for 2 years, and I absolutely love every second we spend together. We do way too much sharing of recipes and feelings, and I'm constantly asking her to feed me these chicken legs whenever I can cajole her into making them. Ironically/Not Ironically, Torri's name means chicken in Japanese, plus she has the thinnest, prettiest little tan chicken legs herself.

She told me to tell you two tricks with this recipe:

1. Make sure you use non-stick foil or else you'll leave your breading behind when removing the chicken from the foil.

2. When dredging and breading the chicken, make sure to do it quickly as the almond flour tends to want to clump up. You'll probably wash your hands halfway through breading the chicken as this can get messy.

Olive oil
1-2 pounds of chicken legs (about 12 legs)
Salt for seasoning
2 eggs
1/4 cup heavy cream
1 1/2 cups almond flour
Hot sauce for garnish

Preheat oven to 400°. Place non-stick foil on a large baking sheet. Drizzle olive oil on the foil.

Season chicken legs with salt. In a shallow bowl, whisk together eggs and heavy cream. Put almond flour into another shallow bowl next to the egg/cream wet batter.

Dredge chicken legs in wet batter, then quickly roll in almond flour, and place on baking sheet. Repeat for all legs. Drizzle a little more olive oil atop each chicken leg.

Bake 30 minutes, and then gently flip chicken with tongs, careful not to pull breading from chicken. Bake an additional 30 minutes until golden brown and crisp. If you'd like it crispier, turn oven off and leave chicken in the oven for an additional 15-20 minutes. Serve with hot sauce.

Chicken with Artichokes, Spinach, and Cherry Tomatoes

(Serves 4)

4 chicken breasts, pounded to 1/2-inch thickness
Salt and pepper for seasoning
1/8 cup olive oil
2 shallots, minced
1 teaspoon butter
1 6-10 ounce jar/can of artichoke hearts, patted dry, quartered, rough tops
trimmed off and discarded
1/2 cup heavy cream
1/2 cup chicken broth
1 cup cherry tomatoes, halved
1-2 cups fresh spinach
1 1/2 cups grated fresh parmesan cheese

Salt and pepper the chicken breast cutlets. Heat up olive oil to medium high heat in sauté pan, cook chicken cutlets all the way through, 6-8 minutes per side. Remove chicken from heat, cover with foil.

In the same sauté pan, cook the minced shallots and butter until softened, about 2 minutes, being careful not to burn. Add in the artichoke hearts, cook for about 3 minutes.

Pour in the heavy cream and chicken broth, bring to a boil, then simmer for 3-4 minutes. Add in the cherry tomatoes and spinach, tossing until coated with the sauce and the spinach wilts, 3-4 minutes.

Remove pan from heat. Mix in parmesan, stir until melted. Place chicken breasts back in sauce, coat them, and then serve.

Lemon Broccoli Chicken

(Serves 3-4)

4 tablespoons olive oil, divided
1 12-ounce bag of broccoli florets, cut into smaller pieces
1 1/4 cups chicken broth
3-4 chicken breasts, trimmed of fat
Salt and pepper for seasoning
1/4 cup coconut flour
1 tablespoon butter
1 shallot, finely chopped
1/2 cup heavy cream
1 teaspoon Worcestershire sauce
Juice of 1/2 lemon
1/2 cup freshly grated parmesan cheese

Heat 2 tablespoons olive oil in a large oven-safe skillet until very hot (but not smoking). Add broccoli and cook until you start to get sear marks, turning after 1 minute. Add 1/4 cup of the chicken broth, cover pan, and cook until broccoli starts to get tender and bright green, about 5 minutes. Place broccoli in a bowl and clean out the skillet.

Season chicken breasts with salt and pepper. Place coconut flour in a shallow bowl, lightly flour the chicken breasts. Heat 2 tablespoons olive oil in your skillet until hot, but not smoking. Cook chicken until browned on each side, about 3-4 minutes per side. Move chicken aside to a plate.

Reduce skillet heat to medium, add in butter and shallots, cooking 30 seconds, but don't let the butter burn. Add in remaining chicken broth, the heavy cream, and Worcestershire sauce. Bring to a boil while scraping up any chicken bits. Return the chicken to the skillet, coating the pieces in the sauce. Let simmer on medium heat for an additional 10 minutes, flipping halfway through.

Turn your broiler onto high. Remove chicken from skillet, cut into smaller pieces. Season your sauce with salt and pepper, continue to cook your sauce until it is reduced and thickened, about 7-8 minutes. Remove the skillet from the heat, whisk in half of the parmesan and the lemon juice. Season again, if necessary, with salt and pepper. Return the chicken and broccoli pieces to the pan and mix into sauce. Sprinkle remaining parmesan on top. Broil for 5-7 minutes until parmesan is golden. Serve immediately.

CHICKEN DIJON

(Serves 4)

Salt and pepper
4 chicken breasts, pounded to 1/2-inch thickness
1/2 cup olive oil
1/4 cup Dijon mustard
2 garlic cloves, loosely chopped
1 teaspoon garlic ~~salt~~
3 slices bacon, cut into 1/2-inch strips
1 sweet onion, thinly sliced
1/2 cup grated Gruyère cheese
5-6 basil leaves, chopped for garnish
Salsa for garnish (optional)

Lightly salt and pepper chicken breasts. Whisk together oil, mustard, garlic, and garlic ~~salt~~. Pour over chicken breasts to coat. Marinate in the fridge 30 minutes to 2 hours.

In cast iron skillet on medium high heat, brown the bacon. Remove bacon from pan onto a plate, reserving fat in pan. In skillet, cook onion slices in reserved bacon fat at medium-high heat until caramelized, about 8-10 minutes. Move onions to bacon plate.

Back in skillet, sauté chicken breasts on medium high heat until cooked through, about 5-7 minutes per side. Top chicken with Gruyère, onions, and bacon pieces. Serve with chopped basil and a dollop of fresh salsa.

Chicken Tikka Masala

(Serves 4-6)

1-2 pounds skinless boneless chicken thighs, cut into 1 1/2-inch pieces
2 1/2 teaspoons salt, divided
1 teaspoon cumin
1 teaspoon cinnamon
2 tablespoons olive oil *divided*
1/2 cup finely chopped onion
1 1/2 tablespoons minced garlic
2 tablespoons minced peeled fresh ginger
1 jalapeño pepper, seeds removed, and minced
1 teaspoon garam masala or make your own (see p. 176)
1/2 teaspoon paprika
1/2 cup chicken broth
1/2 cup heavy cream
2 14.5-ounce cans of chopped tomatoes, undrained
1 cup of cauliflower florets
1 cup green beans cut into 1-inch pieces
2 tablespoons of butter

Sprinkle chicken pieces with 1 teaspoon of the salt, plus the cumin and cinnamon. Heat 1 tablespoon of olive oil in a Le Creuset, or similar large pot, or Dutch oven on medium-high heat. Cook chicken in pot for about 5 minutes or until browned, but not cooked through. Remove chicken from pan and set aside.

Add remaining tablespoon of olive oil to pan and add onion, garlic, ginger, and jalapeño to pan and sauté on medium high heat for about a minute. Reduce to low heat, and cook an additional five minutes or until vegetables are softened. Add garam masala and paprika to pan, and cook for additional minute, stirring constantly. Add remaining 1 1/2 teaspoons of salt, chicken broth, heavy cream, and tomatoes, scraping pan to loosen browned bits. Bring to a boil over high heat. Reduce heat to low and simmer uncovered for 15 minutes.

While sauce is simmering, steam the cauliflower and green beans for about 8 minutes or until tender. When cooked, set aside. Purée sauce in Vitamix® or blender (pulse it for 5-10 seconds or until smooth). Return sauce to Dutch oven. Add chicken and vegetables. Simmer for about 6 minutes or until chicken is cooked through. Add butter to the pot and stir until melted. Serve immediately.

I have lots of ripe lemons to use up on that tree in the back yard. If y'all come over, I'll give you a bushel, I promise. Until then, I'm gonna keep making these simple, inexpensive chicken thighs. The lemon makes the skin taste oh so crispy and melt-in-your-mouth good. Buy thighs with the bone-in and the skin ON, thank you very much.

Lemony Chicken Thighs

(Serves 4-6)

Juice of 2 lemons
1/4 cup olive oil
1 tablespoon sea salt
10-12 bone-in, skin-on chicken thighs
Salt and Pepper for seasoning

Mix the juice of 2 lemons, olive oil, and salt in a large bowl. Toss chicken thighs in the liquid to coat. Marinate for 1-6 hours in the fridge, bringing chicken to room temperature for the last 30 minutes.

Preheat oven to 425°. Remove thighs from the marinade and place them skin-side up in a roasting pan or Pyrex dish. Roast for 45 minutes. Cut into thigh to check for doneness. Clear juices should run from the piercing spot, or the temperature on a meat thermometer should read 175-180°. If not done, pop back in oven for 5 minutes.

Let the chicken rest for 5 minutes before serving. Finish with salt and pepper. Serve immediately.

Fried Sage Leaves
1/2 cup butter or olive oil
20 fresh sage leaves, loosely chopped
Salt

Brown the butter in a small saucepan on low heat. Lay the sage leaves in the pan in the butter. They will cook slowly as the butter warms, becoming crispy in 8-14 minutes. Remove them from the butter gently with a slotted spoon and drain on paper towels. Sprinkle with salt while they are still warm and serve with the chicken.

TARQ'S THAI BASIL CHICKEN AND VEGETABLES

(Serves 4-6)

Adrian Tarquinio is the grilling champ of Leesburg, Virginia, and I'm eternally grateful to him for sharing this recipe with me back when I married his brother...and for sharing countless bottles of Failla Zinfandel ever since.

---

2 pounds boneless chicken breasts
1/2 cup gluten-free soy sauce
1/2 cup fish sauce
1/4 cup garlic chili paste
1/4 cup gluten-free hoisin sauce
6-8 large garlic cloves, peeled and minced
1 bunch of basil, leaves chopped, about 1/4 cup loosely packed
1/2 cup olive oil
1 sweet onion, thickly sliced
4 various colors of bell peppers, thickly sliced

Clean, trim, and cut the chicken breasts into strips. Put the chicken strips into a large plastic baggie.

Whisk together soy sauce, fish sauce, garlic chili paste, hoisin sauce, garlic, basil, and olive oil in medium size bowl. Pour half the marinade into plastic baggie of chicken. Reserve the other half of the marinade. Place the plastic baggie of marinating chicken back in fridge until you are ready to grill.

Split the remaining half of the marinade in half. Refrigerate one portion for serving. Use the other portion to marinate the onion and pepper slices in another large plastic baggie.

Heat up your grill or cast iron pan to medium-high heat. Remove the chicken from the marinade and throw away the bag. Grill the chicken until cooked through.

In a veggie-grilling pan, or separate cast iron pan, grill or sauté the onions and peppers (discarding excess marinade) until soft.

Bring the remaining marinade to room temperature, serve as a dipping sauce or pour over chicken and veggies.

Rotisserie Chicken Salad

(Serves 3-4)

Chicken salad in the summer is an easy go-to lunch favorite. Make this in advance; take it to work in a cooler the next day. I like a regular rotisserie chicken, but some of you prefer the low-sodium chicken. If that's the case, you will need extra seasoning in the dressing, and you can always stir in a little more salt and pepper to the chicken salad if you feel the low-sodium chicken is stealing your seasoning thunder.

Rotisserie chicken, meat pulled and chopped
1 gala apple, peeled, cored, chopped
6 mini cornichons, chopped
3 celery stalks, chopped
1/2 cup olive oil
1 tablespoon mayonnaise
1 teaspoon Dijon mustard
Salt and pepper for seasoning

In a large bowl, fold together the chicken, apple, cornichons, and celery into one mixture.

In a smaller bowl, whisk together olive oil, mayonnaise, Dijon mustard, a dash of salt, and a twist of pepper. Pour over chicken salad and mix together until well-coated.

Moroccan Chicken Stuffed Acorn Squash

(Serves 4)

2 medium acorn squashes, halved lengthwise, and seeds removed
2 tablespoons pine nuts
2 tablespoons olive oil
1/2 medium brown or yellow onion, finely chopped
1 teaspoon minced garlic
2 cups rotisserie chicken, chopped into small pieces
1 teaspoon ground cinnamon
1/2 teaspoon ground nutmeg
1 teaspoon salt
1/2 cup almond flour
1/4 cup water

Preheat oven to 400°. Place squash, cut side down, in a baking dish. Bake until tender, about 45 minutes. Let cool. When cool enough, scoop out the soft flesh of the baked squash, reserving the shells for serving.

In a small non-stick pan, toast pine nuts on high heat, tossing frequently, making sure not to burn. They will toast in 3-4 minutes; then remove from heat.

While the squash bakes, heat olive oil in a large saucepan over medium high heat. Add onion and cook until soft, about 5 minutes. Add garlic and cook for another minute. Add chicken pieces, cinnamon, nutmeg, and 1 teaspoon of salt. Heat the chicken until a little crispy, stirring frequently, about 3-5 minutes.

Preheat oven to 300°. Add almond flour to onion and chicken mixture, stir to combine. Pour in the water and stir. Reduce heat to low, fold in the scooped out squash and the toasted pine nuts, combine. Divide evenly among squash halves, and put back in the oven to bake until tops are browned, about 15 minutes.

FANCY TURKEY BURGERS

(Yield 6–8 patties)

1/8 cup finely sliced green onions
1/3 cup finely chopped celery
1 granny smith apple, peeled and diced
2 tablespoons olive oil for sautéing
1/2 teaspoon of lemon zest
1 pack of ground turkey breast (which is usually 1.25 pounds)
1 teaspoon salt
1 teaspoon freshly ground black pepper
1 teaspoon of Tabasco sauce
Juice of 1/2 lemon
Cheese, Lettuce, Tomato Slices, Avocado Slices for fixins

Sauté the green onions, celery, and apple in 1 tablespoon of the olive oil until soft, about 8 minutes. Let cool. Pour sautéed ingredients and lemon zest into a mini-food processor or blender and purée.

Put the ground turkey into a large mixing bowl. Add the puréed items, salt, pepper, Tabasco, lemon juice, and zest. Mix and form into evenly shaped burgers with an indentation in the middle to prevent the burgers from getting puffy when grilled. Refrigerate for 30 minutes.

Heat grill up to high heat, or heat remaining tablespoon of olive oil to high heat in an iron skillet. Grill each side for 3–4 minutes or until meat is thoroughly cooked. Let sit for 5 minutes. Add cheese and fixins, whatever your pleasure.

EASY TURKEY BURGERS

(Yield 4 patties)

This is a simpler turkey burger recipe, which you can whip up in a pinch on a random Tuesday without having to drag out the food processor or blender. I like to serve these with Nonni's Broccolini when I need to make a 30 minute dinner on the fly.

---

1 pound of ground turkey
2 tablespoons gluten-free soy sauce
1/4 cup organic ketchup
1/2 teaspoon onion powder
1/2 teaspoon garlic powder
1 egg
1 tablespoon olive oil
Large leaves of butter lettuce
Tomato slices
Cheese slices

In a large mixing bowl, combine ground turkey, soy sauce, ketchup, onion powder, garlic powder, and egg. Form into patties with an indentation in the middle to prevent the burgers from getting too puffy. Heat olive oil in a non stick pan to medium high heat, cook burger patties about 5-8 minutes per side until cooked through. Wrap in large butter lettuce leaves, serve with tomato slices and cheese.

TURKEY MEATLOAF

(Serves 3-4)

---

1 pound organic ground turkey
1 medium onion, finely chopped
1/2 can tomato paste (3 ounces)
2 garlic cloves, minced
2 eggs
1 cup almond flour
1/2 teaspoon onion powder
1 teaspoon salt
1/2 teaspoon pepper
1/2 cup grated parmesan
1 teaspoon olive oil to oil the pan

Preheat oven to 350°. In a large mixing bowl, mix ingredients together well by hand. Oil a 4 x 8 meatloaf pan. Place meatloaf mixture in oiled pan and cook for 45-55 minutes, or until done through.

SOUTHERN STYLE TURKEY AND DUMPLINGS STEW

(Serves 4-6)

ROASTED TURKEY BREAST

1 onion, sliced
5-8 sprigs of thyme
1 turkey breast, bone-in, skin on,
  about 2-3 pounds

3 tablespoons butter, cut into thin pats
1 tablespoon olive oil
Salt and pepper
Chicken broth if needed for basting

Preheat oven to 400°. Place onion slices flat on bottom of a 9 x 9 baking dish, topped with the thyme sprigs. Place turkey breast on top of the onion slices. Tuck pats of butter under the skin. Rub 1 tablespoon of olive oil over the turkey skin. Season liberally with salt and pepper. Cook for 60-75 minutes, basting every 15-20 minutes. Add chicken broth to the drippings should the drippings become dry. Cook through; juices should run clear when cutting into it.

Reserve onions from pan, chop and use in the Stew Base (below).

Cut turkey into 1-inch pieces.

STEW BASE

3 stalks celery, chopped
10 baby carrots, chopped
2 tablespoons olive oil
Reserved onions from roasted
  turkey pan, chopped
1/4 teaspoon onion powder
1/4 teaspoon garlic powder

1/2 teaspoon thyme leaves
1/2 cup thin green beans (haricot
  verts), chopped bite size
1/2 teaspoon xanthan gum
3 cups chicken broth
1/4 cup heavy cream

Cook celery and carrots in olive oil on medium-high heat until very soft, about 8-10 minutes. Add in chopped onions, onion powder, garlic powder, thyme leaves, and green beans, mixing evenly. Sprinkle xanthan gum evenly onto mixture. Pour in 3 cups of chicken broth. Bring to a boil. Lower heat and add in turkey pieces. Scoop dumplings by the tablespoon into stew (see below). Cover, let simmer for 25-30 minutes, flipping the dumplings once to make sure they cook all the way through. Turn off heat, add heavy cream.

DUMPLINGS

1 cup almond flour
1/2 cup coconut flour
2 eggs

1 teaspoon salt
1/2 teaspoon pepper
1/4 teaspoon fresh thyme leaves

Mix all ingredients in a bowl until a wet dough forms. When ready, scoop dough out by the tablespoon into the stew above.

Italian Style Turkey Stuffed Green Peppers

(Serves 4-5)

Do you like stuffing things? Do you like peppers? Well, here are some peppers you can stuff with stuff to feed your family and stuff. Use the recipe for Homemade Marinara on p. 172 and cauliflower "rice" to make this a delicious savory grain-free meal.

4-5 green bell peppers (or sweet or spicy pepper of your choice)
1 cup cauliflower florets, stems removed, pulsed in Vitamix® or food processor to create "rice"
1/2 medium yellow or brown onion chopped
3 stalks of celery finely chopped
2 tablespoons of olive oil
1 pound ground turkey

1 teaspoon of salt
1/2 teaspoon onion powder
1/2 teaspoon garlic powder
1/2 teaspoon dried oregano
1/2 teaspoon dried basil
Homemade Marinara Sauce (see p. 172)
1 cup grated mozzarella
Freshly grated parmesan for garnish

Preheat oven to 400°.

Cut the tops off the peppers, scoop out and discard the insides. In a large pot, with enough water to cover the peppers, boil the water, then submerge the peppers, cooking for 10-15 minutes until soft. Remove from water and let cool.

Put cauliflower rice in a bowl, cover with plastic wrap, and microwave for 1 1/2 minutes. Press out excess water with paper towels. Set aside.

In a large sauté pan on medium high heat, cook onions and celery with the olive oil until soft (6-8 minutes). Add turkey and use your spatula to break it up into small bits. Season with the salt, onion powder, garlic powder, oregano, and basil. Stir thoroughly until turkey is cooked through. Remove from heat.

In a large mixing bowl, combine and mix the turkey mixture, 3/4 cup of the marinara, the cauliflower rice, and a half cup of grated mozzarella cheese. Place peppers open side up in an 8 x 8 baking pan. Sprinkle a little cheese into the bottoms of the peppers. Spoon the turkey-cauliflower rice mixture into the green peppers. Top with the remaining mozzarella followed by the rest of the sauce. Bake in the oven 25-30 minutes.

Remove from heat. Let sit for at least 5 minutes. Garnish with freshly grated parmesan and enjoy!

LENTIL BURGERS WITH ZESTIFIED GREEK YOGURT

(Yield 4–5 patties)

These lentil burgers are an easy Meatless Monday option. Serve them lettuce-wrapped with a dollop of Greek yogurt, zestified with hot sauce. You won't miss the meat.

---

1 cup green lentils
4 cups water
1 small sweet onion, cut into chunks
1 cup almond flour, divided
2 eggs, lightly beaten, divided
2 tablespoons chives, chopped
~~4 cups water~~
1 1/2 teaspoons salt, divided
2 tablespoons olive oil
Red Leaf or Bibb lettuce leaves, whole for serving
1 teaspoon hot sauce, such as Tapatio
1/2 cup Greek yogurt

Boil lentils, 1 teaspoon of salt, and 4 cups of water in a saucepan, reduce heat to a simmer and cook until lentils are tender, about 30 minutes. Drain and set aside to cool.

In a Vitamix® or food processor, add half of your lentils, the chunks of onion, 1/2 cup of the almond flour, 1/2 of the beaten eggs, and the chives. Pulse until turned into a paste. Transfer to a big bowl and fold in remaining whole lentils, almond flour, beaten egg, and 1/2 teaspoon salt until well mixed.

Heat 2 tablespoons of olive oil in a non-stick pan over medium high heat. Shape lentil mix into patties, and gently place onto heated pan. The patties will be quite loose due to so much moisture in the mix, so be gentle when placing on the oil so as not to break the shape of the patty.

Cook until crispy and browned, about 3 minutes per side, being careful not to overheat the pan. Serve over whole lettuce leaves. Whisk hot sauce into the Greek yogurt, and put a dollop of the zesty yogurt atop each lentil burger.

Chapter Three: Soups, Casseroles, and Slow Cooker Dishes

PITTSBURGH TURKEY CHILI

(Serves 6-8)

2 tablespoons olive oil
4 celery stalks, thinly chopped
2 garlic cloves, minced

1 large brown onion, finely chopped
2 pounds organic ground turkey
(highest fat possible)

1 tablespoon chili powder
2 teaspoons salt
1/2 teaspoon cinnamon
1/2 teaspoon dried basil
1/2 teaspoon dried oregano

1/2 teaspoon ground allspice
1/2 teaspoon ground cumin
1/2 teaspoon fresh ground black
pepper

3 14-ounce cans organic diced
tomatoes, puréed in Vitamix®
1/2 of a 6-ounce can organic tomato
paste

1 tablespoon red wine vinegar
1 chicken bouillon cube
1/2 ounce dark chocolate, finely
chopped

For extra veggies, you can add:
4oz can artichoke hearts, drained and chopped
2 zucchini, sliced

For garnish:
2 cups grated Colby Jack or cheddar cheese
Crème fraîche or sour cream

In a large pot, Le Creuset, Dutch oven, or slow cooker, heat olive oil. When shimmering, add the celery, garlic, and the chopped onion and sauté until softened. Add turkey, breaking up lumps of meat, until it loses its pink color.

Mix together chili powder, salt, cinnamon, basil, oregano, allspice, cumin, and pepper in a little bowl until well blended. Add this dry spice mix to the turkey. Cook and stir for about a minute.

Add the puréed tomatoes, tomato paste, red wine vinegar, the optional veggies, bouillon cube and the chocolate. Bring to a boil, then reduce heat to low. Cover and let simmer for about an hour.

Uncover and stir, letting chili simmer for another 1/2 hour.

Place the grated cheese and crème fraîche in separate bowls. Serve chili and let everyone choose their own toppings.

If Making In A Slow Cooker:

Sauté the onions, garlic, and celery, then brown the turkey in a sauté pan. Mix together all dry spices in a little bowl until well blended. Add the dry spice mix to the turkey, cook and stir for about a minute. Transfer mixture to the slow cooker and add the remaining ingredients, stir. Cook on the high setting for 2 hours. Serve.

Quesadilla Casserole

(Serves 4)

---

1 pound ground beef or turkey
Homemade Taco Seasoning (see p. 178)
1/4 cup water
2 tablespoons olive oil
1 onion, thinly sliced (or use Lime-Soaked Onions p. 181)
1 red bell pepper, thinly sliced
1 cup cremini mushrooms, chopped
1 cup fresh spinach
1/4 cup fire roasted mild green chiles
1/4 cup red salsa
1 cup grated Mexican blend cheese
Garnish with Greek yogurt and salsa

Preheat oven to 350°. In a large sauté pan, brown ground meat, breaking up into small bits as it cooks. Drain, place back into pan, add Homemade Taco Seasoning, and 1/4 cup of water. Mix and reduce heat to low, letting sauté for an additional 5-10 minutes.

Meanwhile, in another sauté pan, heat the olive oil on medium high heat. Sauté the onion and pepper until soft, about 8 minutes. Add mushrooms, sauté until soft, another 5-6 minutes. Add spinach, green chiles, and salsa. Mix until spinach is wilted. Remove from heat.

Place the ground meat in an 8 x 8 casserole dish. Cover with a thin sprinkling of cheese. Then top with the vegetable mix, spreading it out evenly. Top with remaining cheese and bake in oven for 15 minutes, or until cheese is melted and bubbly. Remove from oven and let stand 10 minutes before serving. Garnish with Greek yogurt and salsa.

Slow Cooked Tri-Tip

(Serves 4-6)

This addictively tender and juicy version of a pot roast is based on my Aunt Diane's recipe for Hot Beef with Bread, a staple of hers in Kenosha, Wisconsin, that she would make every Sunday for the Packers game. She taught it to me when I first got married. I tinkered with it over the years—including losing the bread part of the recipe. The beef part of Hot Beef is pretty darn good on its own.

2-3 pound tri-tip roast
Salt and pepper to season the roast
1/2 cup water
1 beef bouillon cube
1/2 teaspoon garlic salt
1 tablespoon Worcestershire sauce
1 tablespoon Dijon mustard
1/2 teaspoon dried oregano
1 onion, sliced

Thoroughly salt and pepper the roast. Combine all remaining ingredients in the slow cooker, and place roast on top. Cook on high for 4-5 hours or low for 8-10 hours. Remove meat and onions from the slow cooker, reserving the leftover jus. Pull apart with fork. Serve with the onions and jus from the slow cooker.

Slow Cooked Pot Roast

(Serves 4-6)

=====================================

4 pound roast (chuck roast, bottom round roast, or tri-tip roast)
Salt and pepper
2 tablespoons olive oil
2 tablespoons Dijon mustard
1 onion, loosely chopped
10 baby carrots
3 celery stalks chopped
1 cup beef or chicken broth
1 tablespoon red wine vinegar

=====================================

Rub the entire roast with salt and pepper. Heat olive oil in a sauté pan to medium high heat and brown all sides of the roast, about 3 minutes per side. Remove roast from heat, set aside. Reserve drippings in sauté pan and pour into a slow cooker.

Glaze browned roast with the Dijon mustard. Place veggies into the slow cooker, then the roast on top. Pour in broth and Red Wine Vinegar. Add an additional dash of salt and pepper.

Cover and cook in slow cooker on low for 8-10 hours or on high for 4-6 hours.

SLOW COOKED BRISKET

(Serves 4-6)

1 large yellow or brown onion, sliced
Salt and pepper
3-4 pound brisket (get a brisket as large as can fit in your slow cooker because they shrink)
1/4 cup olive oil
1/4 cup gluten-free soy sauce
1 6-ounce can tomato paste
1/2 cup water
1/2 bouillon cube, smashed into powder (chicken, beef, or veggie is fine)
1 teaspoon dried mustard
2 tablespoons red wine vinegar
1/2 teaspoon onion powder
1/2 teaspoon garlic powder

Place onion slices in a layer in bottom of slow cooker. Rub salt and pepper into the brisket. Lay brisket atop onion slices, fat side facing up.

Whisk together remaining ingredients until you've made a sauce with a ketchup-like consistency. Pour over brisket. Cook on low in slow cooker for 8 hours.

If you don't have a slow cooker, you can use a Dutch oven. Combine all ingredients above, cover, and cook in oven at 250° for 8 hours.

Slow Cooked Short Ribs

(Serves 4-6)

2-4 pounds boneless short ribs, trimmed of excess fat
Salt and pepper to season ribs
1 teaspoon smoked paprika
1 teaspoon minced garlic (or 2 garlic cloves, minced)
1 teaspoon fresh oregano, chopped (okay to use 1 teaspoon dried oregano)
1 tablespoon red wine vinegar
1/2 cup ketchup
1 tablespoon mustard
1 teaspoon gluten-free soy sauce
Pinch smoky Hawaiian black salt (found in specialty markets, sea salt is great, too)
3-4 sprigs of fresh thyme

Season short ribs with salt and pepper. Place ribs in a slow cooker.

In a bowl, whisk remaining ingredients except for thyme sprigs into a sauce. Pour over ribs and dredge ribs in the sauce, then place thyme springs on top. Cook on high in covered slow cooker for 3 hours or until ribs are fall-apart tender. Remove thyme sprigs before serving.

Fall Off the Bone BBQ Ribs

(Serves 4-6)

2 pounds country style ribs, bone-in (or a rack of pork loin back ribs)
Salt and pepper
1 onion, thinly sliced
1/2 teaspoon garlic powder
1/2 teaspoon onion powder
1 cup chicken broth

Salt and pepper the ribs. Heat a nonstick pan to high heat, brown both sides of the ribs. Place ribs in slow cooker with onion slices, garlic powder, onion powder, and chicken broth. Cook on high for 4-6 hours or low 8-10 hours until rib meat is tender and falling off the bone.

Serve rib meat with Barbecue Sauce (see p. 170).

Pulled Pork BBQ

(Serves 8-10)

2 medium onions, sliced
1 tablespoon paprika
2 teaspoons salt
1/2 teaspoon freshly ground pepper
3-4 pound boneless pork butt roast
3/4 cup apple cider vinegar
4 teaspoons Worcestershire sauce
1 teaspoon red pepper flakes
1/2 teaspoon dried mustard
1/2 teaspoon garlic salt
1/4 teaspoon cayenne pepper
1/4-1/2 cup Barbecue Sauce (see p. 170)
Red Cabbage and Kale Slaw (see p. 147)
Pickles for serving

Place sliced onions at the bottom of a slow cooker.

Combine paprika, salt and pepper into a dry rub. Rub all over the roast. Place roast atop the onions in a slow cooker.

Combine vinegar, Worcestershire sauce, red pepper flakes, mustard, garlic salt, and cayenne, whisking well to blend. Drizzle vinegar mixture over roast. Cover the slow cooker and cook on low for 10-12 hours.

Remove pork and onions from the slow cooker and place into a bowl. Shred the pork with two forks. Pour on your favorite barbecue sauce to taste. Serve with Red Cabbage and Kale Slaw and pickles.

PORK CHILI VERDE

(Serves 8–10)

2 tablespoons olive oil
1 sweet onion, chopped
3–4 pound pork sirloin roast, shoulder, or butt, trimmed of excess fat and
cubed into 1-inch pieces
1 cup Green Salsa (see p. 182)
2 cups chicken broth
Salt and pepper
Avocado slices, chopped cilantro, and crème fraîche for garnish
Lime slices for serving

Heat olive oil on medium high heat in large stock pot or cast iron pot, sauté onions until soft, 3–5 minutes. Brown pork pieces for 4–5 minutes, flipping the pieces until all sides are browned. Add salsa and broth, bring to boil, season with salt and pepper. Lower heat to a simmer for 1 hour. Season three to four times with salt and pepper throughout cooking to desired flavor.

Garnish with avocado slices, chopped cilantro, and a dollop of crème fraîche and serve with lime slices.

CHEESY ZUCCHINI BAKE

(Serves 4)

1 tablespoon olive oil
1 tablespoon butter
1-2 shallots, chopped
1 red pepper, chopped
Pinch garlic salt
Pinch dried oregano
Butter to grease the pan
3-4 zucchini, sliced into disks (I use a Mandoline slicer)
Salt and pepper
1/3 cup full fat ricotta cheese
2 cups grated Colby Jack cheese
1/4 cup heavy cream

Preheat oven to 350°.

Heat up olive oil and butter in non-stick sauté pan at medium-high heat. Throw in shallots and cook 3-5 minutes until they start to caramelize. Add in red pepper, garlic salt, and oregano. Cook a few more minutes until shallots are caramelized and the red peppers are soft. Remove from heat and set aside.

Grease a 9 x 12 pan with butter. Place zucchini disks, one layer at a time, spreading them apart fairly evenly like you would do with scalloped potatoes. Salt and pepper each new layer of zucchini. Spread the ricotta cheese over the first layer of zucchini. On the second layer, sprinkle a handful of the grated cheese. On the third layer, evenly pour the heavy cream, and on the fourth layer spread out the shallot and pepper mixture. Top with remainder of grated cheese.

Bake 30 minutes at 350°, or until the top is slight browned and bubbly.

Sausage Zucchini Bake

(Serves 4)

What if we take the basic Zucchini Bake recipe and add some leftovers from the Sausage Stuffed Mushrooms recipe? The answer: Sausage Zucchini Bake, a recipe that has taken on a life and a reputation all its own. This dish is such a crowd pleaser, I have to double the recipe and use two casserole dishes to satisfy the thronging masses.

---

2 tablespoons olive oil
1 small onion, chopped
1 red bell pepper, chopped
1/2 pound cremini or button mushrooms, chopped
1 pound of your favorite sausage; discard any casing
1 tablespoon red wine vinegar
1/3 cup almond flour
1/4 cup Boursin cheese (the original firm cheese, not the soft spread)
3-4 zucchini, sliced into discs
Butter for greasing a 9 x 12 baking pan
Salt and pepper for seasoning
2 cups grated Colby Jack or cheddar cheese

In a large sauté pan, heat olive oil on medium high heat. Cook onions and peppers 3-4 minutes until soft. Add mushrooms, sauté an additional 5-6 minutes until soft. Move onion, pepper, and mushroom mixture to the outer perimeter of the pan. Add sausage, breaking it into small bits as it browns. Drain any excess grease after browning sausage.

Sprinkle in red wine vinegar, stir. Sprinkle on almond flour, stir in evenly. Remove from heat and add Boursin cheese, folding into mixture evenly until creamy. In the pan, divide mixture into thirds, set aside to prep zucchini.

Meanwhile, preheat oven to 350°. Wash zucchini and slice into discs, using a knife, Mandoline, or food processor with the slicing attachment. Grease a 9 x 12 baking pan with a thin coat of butter. Lay out one layer of zucchini, in a scalloped pattern, edge over edge in rows. Season with salt and pepper. Spread out one third of sausage mixture. Top with one third of grated cheese. Repeat with two more layers of zucchini, seasoning, sausage mixture, and cheese until all ingredients are in the casserole pan.

Cover with foil, bake at 350° for 30 minutes. Remove foil and bake another 15 minutes or until cheese is golden and bubbly.

Eggplant Parmesan Casserole

(Serves 4–6)

2 large eggplants cut into 1/2 inch disks
Salt and pepper
1 cup almond flour
2 tablespoons Italian flat leaf parsley, finely chopped
1 teaspoon garlic salt
Homemade Marinara (see p. 172)
8 ounces shredded mozzarella cheese
1/2 cup grated parmesan

Prepare the eggplant by "sweating" it: sprinkle salt on both sides of the eggplant pieces. Let salted eggplant slices sit spread out on a cookie sheet for 15–20 minutes while making the marinara.

Preheat oven to 400°. In a shallow bowl, whisk together the almond flour, chopped parsley, and garlic salt. Dip the eggplant pieces in the almond flour mixture. They will be "sweaty" from sitting with salt on them. This excess water will help the almond flour mixture stick to the eggplant slices.

Pour enough marinara into a buttered casserole dish to coat the bottom. Lay out the coated eggplant slices. Pour a thin layer of marinara over the eggplant pieces. Cover with a half of the mozzarella and parmesan. Continue with a second layer of eggplant pieces until all are in the pan. Top with another handful of cheese sprinkled evenly over the top.

Bake for 30 minutes or until the cheese bubbles and starts to turn golden.

HEARTY TOMATO STEW

(Serves 4–8)

3 tablespoons olive oil
2 carrots, chopped
1 small onion, chopped
1 clove garlic, minced
1 zucchini, sliced
1/2 teaspoon red pepper flakes
1/2 teaspoon salt
1/2 teaspoon freshly ground black pepper
1 26-ounce jar marinara sauce or Homemade Marinara (see p. 172)
2 cups chicken broth
Parmesan for serving

Warm the olive oil in a large soup pot over medium-high heat. Add the carrots, onion, and garlic and cook them until soft, about 3–5 minutes. Add the zucchini, red pepper flakes, salt, and pepper and mix. Add the marinara sauce and chicken broth. Simmer for 30 minutes to thicken into a heartier soup. Ladle into bowls and serve with freshly grated parmesan.

Roasted Lentil and Cauliflower Soup

(Serves 4-6)

2 tablespoons olive oil
1/2 large onion, finely chopped
4 stalks of celery, finely chopped
1 medium carrot, finely chopped
3 sprigs thyme (plus more for garnish)
Salt and pepper
1/2 teaspoon garlic powder
1/2 teaspoon onion powder
1/2 teaspoon dried oregano

1/2 teaspoon dried basil
1 cup green lentils, rinsed and drained
1 32-ounce box of chicken broth
  or use homemade
1 12-ounce bag of cauliflower
  florets, cut into small pieces
1/2 cup of grated smoked Gouda
  cheese
1/2 cup of grated parmesan

Heat oil in a large pot or Dutch oven over medium-high heat. Add onion, celery, carrot, and thyme. Season with salt and pepper, garlic powder, onion powder, dried oregano, and dried basil. Stir occasionally, and cook for approximately 8 minutes or until the vegetables are soft. Add lentils and broth; bring to a boil. Reduce heat, cover, and simmer until lentils are tender, about 30 minutes. Stir in cauliflower, increase heat to medium-high heat. Simmer just until cauliflower is tender, about 3 minutes. Remove thyme stems and season with salt and pepper to taste.

Preheat broiler with rack 6 inches from heating element. Divide soup among 4 broiler proof ramekins or soup bowls. Top with cheese and broil until golden and bubbling, 3-4 minutes. Garnish with thyme and serve immediately.

Jackie's Split Pea Soup

(Serves 6–8)

Jackie is the beautiful woman who used to hold my life together. But Jackie's now a new mommy of the cutest little baby boy with the cutest name ever: Axel! He's a heartbreaker in the making. Now that Jackie is busy with motherhood, she left me with the most delicious split pea soup recipe that I've ever tasted. [Translation: I stole it from her, and I'm hoping she doesn't notice.]

1 medium onion, diced
3 celery stalks, chopped
1/2 cup baby carrots, chopped
2 tablespoons olive oil
Salt and pepper
1/2 teaspoon onion powder
1/2 teaspoon dried thyme
1 teaspoon oregano
5 garlic cloves, minced

1 16-ounce bag of dried split peas, rinsed thoroughly
2 32-ounce boxes of chicken broth or use homemade
3 bay leaves
1 ham steak, preferably bone-in
Grated cheddar cheese and sour cream for garnish (optional)

In a large pot or Dutch oven, sauté onion, celery, and carrots in olive oil on medium high heat until soft, about 8–10 minutes. Season with salt and pepper, stir. Add in onion powder, dried thyme, dried oregano, and minced garlic, then stir. Add in rinsed split peas, chicken broth, and bay leaves. Bring to a boil. Add ham steak. Lower heat to simmer. Cover and cook for 2 hours. Find and discard bay leaves. Remove ham steak, and cut into small cubes. Return the ham to the soup. If you want an extra smooth soup, you can purée in blender while you are cutting the ham steak, but this is not necessary. Serve with optional cheddar cheese and sour cream garnish, or keep it dairy free and serve the soup on its own.

Low Carb Vichyssoise

(Serves 2-4)

This vichyssoise replaces the humble potato with our versatile friend cauliflower. It's every bit as rich and satisfying and velvety smooth as its starchy grand-mère.

---

1 sweet onion, sliced thinly
2 leeks, washed well and sliced thinly
12-ounce bag of cauliflower florets (or one crown of cauliflower), chopped
1 teaspoon salt
1/2 teaspoon pepper
1/2 teaspoon onion powder
1/2 teaspoon garlic powder
2 cups chicken broth
1/2 cup heavy cream
Olive oil for garnish

In a large sauté pan on medium high heat, sauté the onions, leeks, and cauliflower in the olive oil, about 10 minutes. Add salt, pepper, onion powder, and garlic powder and mix thoroughly. Pour in chicken broth, bring to boil, cover and reduce heat to let veggies steam for 15–20 minutes until soft.

Transfer contents to Vitamix® or blender. Blend on soup setting for 5 minutes. After 4 minutes, pour heavy cream, let blend one more minute. Serve hot in winter and cold in summer. Drizzle with olive oil.

Note: If you don't have a Vitamix® or similar blender, you can use an immersion blender in your sauté pan and pass the contents through a strainer so the vichyssoise turns out velvety smooth.

CHICKEN SAGE SOUP

(Serves 4-6)

This is a version of chicken noodle soup that makes you never miss the noodles. You can use leftover chicken from the Easiest Roast Chicken recipe or a rotisserie chicken to keep the prep time under 30 minutes. Save the chicken carcass to make broth for your next chicken soup.

---

1 tablespoon olive oil
1 yellow onion, chopped
3 stalks celery, chopped
2 carrots, peeled and chopped
1/2 teaspoon dried oregano
1/2 teaspoon dried basil
1/2 teaspoon dried thyme
1/2 teaspoon onion powder
1/2 teaspoon garlic powder
12 sage leaves, chopped
4 cups chicken broth (or one box if using store bought)
1 rotisserie chicken, light and dark meat pulled and/or cut into 1/2-inch pieces
Freshly grated parmesan cheese for garnish

In a large Dutch oven pot or Le Creuset, heat olive oil to medium high heat until shimmering. Sauté onions, celery, and carrots until very soft, about 8-10 minutes. Add in oregano, basil, thyme, onion powder, and garlic powder, mix in well with vegetables. Add in sage leaves, cook for an additional 3-5 minutes. Pour in chicken broth. Let come to boil, then reduce to simmer. Add in chicken and cook for 15-20 minutes. Serve immediately and garnish with fresh parmesan cheese.

HOMEMADE CHICKEN BROTH

(Yields 8-10 cups)

Chicken broth is like the little black dress of your kitchen. It never goes out of style, and you can throw it on for pretty much any occasion. With every single chicken that I roast, I use the leftover carcass to make chicken broth. The recipe below is basic, but will yield a ton of flavor much deeper and more intense than any store-bought broth. You can substitute any herb or veggie you like: mushrooms, fennel, leeks, parsnips, garlic, shallots, or whatever you have on hand that you'd like to try. A bouquet garni is a tied up little bundle of fresh herbs (please tie with actual kitchen string, Bridget Jones). Or you can just throw them in there loosely. Or just use a teaspoon each of the dried herb version. Are you getting the "this is easy to make" vibe? It is!

1 roasted chicken carcass
8 baby carrots
2 celery stalks, chopped twice
1 medium onion quartered (you can leave the skin on if you'd like—experiment!)
1 bay leaf
1 bouquet garni of herbs on hand; I use oregano, thyme, and sage
2 teaspoons salt
1 teaspoon fresh pepper
1 tablespoon apple cider vinegar
Enough water to cover the entire chicken in a large stock pot

Place all ingredients in large pot. Bring to a boil, then turn down and let simmer 3-4 hours. A few times during cooking, use a wooden spoon to smash down the chicken bones. Drain broth through a colander, and let cool for a 1/2 hour. Pour broth through a strainer to remove remaining debris. Pour into freezer ware and freeze, or keep refrigerated for up to 5 days.

ALBONDIGAS KALE SOUP

(Serves 6–8)

Meatballs
1 pound 80/20 ground beef (I use ground sirloin)
1/3 cup almond flour
1 egg, beaten
1 tablespoon fresh mint, minced
1 teaspoon salt
Pinch of cumin

Soup
1 tablespoon olive oil
1/2 onion, finely chopped
2 garlic cloves, minced
2 boxes of chicken broth (or 8 cups of homemade broth if you have it on hand)
2 chicken bouillon cubes
1 can of tomatoes, chopped (reserve juices)
2 cups loosely chopped kale
4–6 baby carrots, sliced
Salt and pepper for seasoning

Place all meatball ingredients in a large bowl and combine evenly with your hands. Form into meatballs, about 1 inch to 1 1/2-inches in diameter.

In a Le Creuset or Dutch oven, sauté the onions in the oil until soft. Add the garlic and continue sautéing an additional 3–5 minutes. Add the chicken broth and bouillon cubes and bring to a boil, making sure the bouillon cubes dissolve thoroughly. Place meatballs in the broth and bring to a boil again. Skim the foam off the top of the soup occasionally.

Reduce the heat to medium-low, add in the tomatoes and reserved juices. Cover and simmer for 20 minutes.

Add in the kale and carrots, cover, and simmer for another 20–30 minutes, seasoning with salt and pepper if necessary.

SIMPLE BEEF & PORTOBELLO STEW

(Serves 4-6)

You don't have to be a simpleton to gobble down some Simple Beef & Portobello Stew. Know how to make it even simpler? Use a slow cooker. This tomato based stew uses grass-fed beef and portobello mushrooms for a heartiness that will stick to your ribs. The slow cooker makes it all happen without any fuss. Family is happy ... boom goes the dynamite.

---

1 pound grass fed beef stew meat, cut into chunks
1/2 teaspoon onion powder to season beef
1 yellow onion, loosely chopped
3 stalks celery, loosely chopped
1/2 cup loosely chopped carrots
8 ounces portobello mushroom caps, loosely chopped (about 3-4 portobello caps)
1 14-ounce can diced tomatoes
3 ounces tomato paste (1/2 can)
1/2 cup chicken broth
1 tablespoon red wine vinegar
1/2 teaspoon dried oregano
1/2 teaspoon dried thyme
1 teaspoon salt, plus more for seasoning
1/2 teaspoon ground pepper, plus more for seasoning

Season beef with onion powder. Brown on high heat in a sauté pan, searing each side of the beef chunks, about 3-4 minutes total. Pour beef into slow cooker; add in all remaining ingredients. Cook on low 8-10 hours or high 4-5 hours until stew is ready, season with additional salt and pepper to taste.

Asparagus, Onion, and Mushroom Cream Soup

(Serves 2-3)

The blender or Vitamix® is key to the creaminess of this soup. Pouring in the heavy cream at the end makes the soup decadent and filling. You will have no idea that you're eating a high volume of vegetables.

1 pound asparagus
1 medium onion, chopped
1 pound cremini, baby bella, or button mushrooms
1 1/2 cups chicken or vegetable broth
1 teaspoon salt
1/2 teaspoon freshly ground pepper
1/2 cup heavy cream

Cut and discard the rough ends of the asparagus, usually the bottom 2-3 inches of the stalk. Cut the remaining asparagus into 2-inch pieces.

In a steamer basket, steam the asparagus, onion, and mushrooms for 5-7 minutes, until tender. Simultaneously, heat up the chicken broth until boiling. Remove from heat.

In a blender or Vitamix®, purée the vegetables, chicken broth, salt, and pepper for 3-4 minutes, until smooth. Add in heavy cream and pulse to blend it in until smooth. Serve immediately.

Chapter Four: Sides

BACON BROCCOLI

(Serves 3-4)

1 bundle of broccoli crowns, cut into smaller florets
(or buy bag of pre-cut broccoli florets)
2 tablespoons raw pine nuts
3-4 slices of bacon, cut into 1/2-inch pieces
1 teaspoon garlic salt
1 teaspoon lemon juice or the juice from 1/2 small lemon
2 tablespoons olive oil
Pepper and fresh parmesan for seasoning at the end (optional)

Preheat oven to 400°. Line a large baking sheet with foil for easy clean up.

In a bowl combine broccoli florets, pine nuts, and bacon pieces, adding in garlic salt and lemon juice evenly. Pour olive oil over the broccoli mixture. Combine with hands to make sure all the broccoli florets get some olive oil.

Pour broccoli mixture onto baking sheet and spread out evenly as the bacon will have a tendency to stick together.

Bake for 40 minutes, flipping and rearranging broccoli every 10 minutes, until broccoli looks roasted and bacon is crispy. If you don't flip the mixture, you will burn the broccoli florets.

Season with optional pepper and a dash of freshly grated parmesan.

BROCCOLI WITH LEMON CREAM SAUCE

(Serves 3-4)

---

1 crown of broccoli cut into small pieces or a 12-ounce bag of broccoli
1/2 teaspoon garlic salt
1/4 cup slivered almonds
2 tablespoons butter
1 large or 2 small finely chopped shallots
1 tablespoon lemon juice
1 teaspoon lemon zest, finely minced
2 tablespoons heavy cream

Place broccoli in a steaming basket, sprinkle with garlic salt, and steam broccoli for about 10 minutes or until tender.

Toast the almonds in a pan for 3-5 minutes stirring constantly to make sure you don't burn the almonds. Remove from heat and put aside.

Wipe pan clean with a towel, and heat butter until bubbly. Add minced shallots, and cook on medium high heat until soft for about 3 minutes being careful not to burn the shallots. Add the lemon juice and lemon zest. Cook for another couple minutes. Remove pan from heat. Add the toasted almonds and heavy cream, stirring until mixed. Toss with broccoli and serve.

SPRING VEGGIE SAUTÉ

(Serves 3-4)

---

1 tablespoon olive oil
1 leek, chopped
8 mini peppers, sliced
Head of broccoli, cut into smaller pieces
Juice from 1 lemon
Salt and pepper for seasoning
Freshly grated parmesan for serving (optional)

In a large sauté pan, heat olive oil to medium high heat. Add in leeks and peppers, and cook for 4-5 minutes until soft, being careful not to burn the delicate leeks. Add in broccoli pieces, tossing with peppers and leeks. Squeeze lemon juice over veggies, cover, and turn heat to low. Steam veggies for 5-7 minutes, or until broccoli is green and tender. Season with salt and pepper, and serve with a dusting of freshly grated parmesan.

NONNI'S BROCCOLINI

(Serves 2-4)

1 pound broccolini
8 cloves garlic
1/3 cup olive oil
Salt

Wash the broccolini, leave it wet. With a veggie peeler, peel away the rough skin on the outside of the bottom of the broccolini stalk. Cut garlic cloves into chunks, not too small or else they will burn. In a flat, wide sauté pan, heat olive oil on medium high for 3-5 minutes. Oil is hot enough when you sprinkle water and it sizzles. Place broccolini, garlic, and a pinch of salt in pan. Cover, cook for 10 minutes, stirring once. Turn heat to medium low heat. Cook 10 minutes more, stirring once.

Lemon Oregano Zucchini Pasta with Cauliflower
(Serves 3-4)

The lightness of this dish makes it a perfect side dish. Or plop a ton of it in a giant bowl, smother it in parmesan, and gobble the whole thing up.

2 tablespoons olive oil
1 teaspoon lemon zest, finely minced
1 teaspoon fresh thyme leaves
2 tablespoons fresh oregano leaves, loosely chopped
3 tablespoons capers
12-ounce bag cauliflower florets
2 tablespoons pine nuts
Juice of 1/2 lemon
1 pound zucchini, spiralized
Salt and pepper for seasoning
Fresh parmesan for garnish (optional)

In a large sauté pan on medium high heat, toss lemon zest, thyme, oregano, and capers in pan for 3-4 minutes. Add cauliflower florets, pine nuts, and lemon juice, tossing cauliflower florets to coat. Season with salt and pepper, then let cook for 3-4 minutes, stirring cauliflower every so often so as not to burn it.

Add in spiraled zucchini, toss to coat, and season again with salt and pepper. Cover, cook for 8-10 minutes until zucchini is tender. Toss contents of pan once more, garnish with fresh parmesan (optional), and serve.

Spicy Zucchini Pasta with Pesto

(Serves 4)

2 tablespoons olive oil
2 bell peppers, chopped
2 leeks, chopped finely
1 pint of cherry tomatoes, halved
8 slices of hard salami, sliced into strips
1/2 teaspoon red pepper flakes
Salt and pepper
3-4 zucchini, spiralized
Parmesan for garnish
Homemade Pesto for garnish (see p. 175)

Heat olive oil in a large sauté pan on medium high heat. Add bell peppers and sauté until softened. Add leeks, cherry tomatoes, and salami and sauté until softened. Leeks will be almost caramelized. Sprinkle in red pepper flakes and season with salt and pepper.

Gently fold in the zucchini, tossing to coat with sautéed mixture. Season again with salt and pepper. Cover and cook for another 10-15 minutes, until zucchini is steamed through. Season once again with salt and pepper if necessary. Toss zucchini pasta once more before serving, garnish with fresh parmesan and a dollop of Homemade Pesto.

Zucchini Béchamel Mac & Cheese

(Serves 6-8)

5 slices of pancetta, diced
1 stick of butter
2 cups almond flour
3-4 zucchini, washed with tops cut off (about 1 pound)
3 cups whole milk
3 tablespoons arrowroot starch
Salt and pepper for seasoning
2 cups grated mozzarella cheese
3 cups grated cheddar cheese
3 cups grated Gruyère cheese
2 cups grated Fontina cheese

Heat sauté pan on medium high heat. Add pancetta, lower heat to medium and cook until crispy and lightly browned, about 8-10 minutes, being careful not to burn. Remove pancetta with slotted spoon to rest on a paper towel.

In remaining pancetta drippings, melt 1/3 stick of butter. When melted, add the almond flour and toss until fully mixed. The almond flour will brown slightly as you cook for 7-8 minutes, turning often with a spatula to keep from burning. Transfer to a plate.

Using your Paderno Spiralizer, spiralize the zucchini. Give the pile of spiralized zucchini 6 or 7 chops to break up the longer ribbons of zucchini.

Heat milk in small saucepan until steaming (do not let milk scald or boil).

Preheat oven to 350°, grease a 9 x 12 baking pan with butter. In a separate large sauté pan, melt remaining butter (2/3 stick) over medium heat. Add arrowroot starch to butter, whisking until smooth. Add 1/2 teaspoon of salt. Add milk slowly, whisking constantly until combined. Reduce heat to a simmer and cook, whisking every other minute to break up any clumps that may form, until thickened, about 10 minutes. Season with one more teaspoon of salt and a dash pepper.

Turn off heat. Fold in grated cheeses one at a time, using a spatula to blend. The cheese sauce will seem gummy, but keep folding in the cheese until it's melted. Fold in spiralized zucchini to coat with cheese sauce. Pour into baking dish. Sprinkle pancetta pieces on top, then spread almond flour mixture evenly on top.

Cover with foil and bake for 30 minutes. Remove foil and bake an additional 15 minutes.

Zucchini Dijon Sauté

(Serves 4)

---

2 tablespoons olive oil
1 small onion, chopped
1 red pepper, chopped
3-4 zucchini peeled and sliced evenly into disks
2 tablespoons Dijon mustard
1 tablespoon butter
Salt and pepper for seasoning
1 cup cherry or grape tomatoes, halved
2 tablespoons fresh basil, chopped
Parmesan, freshly grated (optional)

Heat olive oil to medium high heat in a large, flat bottomed pan. Sauté onions and peppers until very soft, about 8 minutes.

Add zucchini, Dijon mustard, tablespoon of butter, salt, and pepper, stirring until everything is pretty evenly coated. Cover. Lower heat to medium-low and let simmer for 5-8 minutes, or until zucchini softens.

Stir in the tomatoes and basil, re-cover the pan and simmer an additional 10 minutes. Remove cover, turn off heat, and add freshly grated parmesan to taste.

LEMONY SPINACH

(Serves 2)

---

3 tablespoons butter
1 minced garlic clove
Juice of 1/2 a Meyer lemon
1/4 cup heavy cream
6-10 ounce bag of baby spinach
Salt and pepper to taste

In a large sauté pan on medium high heat, melt butter until bubbly, but not browning. Add garlic, stirring so that garlic does not burn. Add in lemon juice. Continue to cook and stir another 2 minutes. Lower heat to medium low. Add in heavy cream and whisk until combined.

Pour entire bag of baby spinach into pan. Toss spinach in the lemon-cream mixture until spinach begins to wilt. Season with salt and pepper and serve immediately.

CREAMED SPINACH

(Serves 4-6)

3 tablespoons butter, plus more to grease 9 x 12 pan
1 onion, chopped
1 teaspoon minced garlic (2 cloves)
2 cups heavy cream
1 cup half and half
1/4 teaspoon nutmeg
1 tablespoon Dijon mustard
1 teaspoon salt, plus more for extra seasoning
1/2 teaspoon pepper
1 6-ounce bag of fresh spinach, chopped
2 pounds frozen spinach, thawed and thoroughly dried (this step is essential)
2 cups grated Gruyère cheese

Topping:
1/2 cup grated Gruyère cheese
1/2 cup almond flour
1/2 teaspoon salt

Preheat oven to 400°. Heat butter on medium high heat in a wide, flat sauté pan and cook onions until soft, about 7-9 minutes. Add garlic, cook an additional 2 minutes. Whisk in cream and half and half, nutmeg, Dijon mustard, salt, and pepper. Bring to boil then reduce to simmer for 10 minutes, whisking every few minutes to make sure there is no sticking. Fold in the chopped fresh spinach. Cook 2-3 minutes until wilted. Add in one more dash of salt and pepper. Fold in the frozen spinach, cook for 2-3 minutes. Remove pan from heat. Fold in 2 cups of the grated Gruyère until melted. Pour mixture into a well-greased 9 x 12 baking pan.

Mix together the topping ingredients in a small bowl. Pour the topping over the spinach evenly. Bake 20-30 minutes or until browned on top and bubbling.

Roasted Asparagus with Manchego and Pine Nuts

(Serves 4)

Quick tip: when prepping the asparagus, wash and dry, then bend the spears until you feel the natural snapping point at the bottom, then snap off the tough ends to make sure you are serving only the tender part of the asparagus.

Asparagus roasts so easily, keep an eye on those delicate suckers so they don't burn.

1 pound fresh asparagus, ends snapped off
Drizzle of olive oil
Three lemon slices, plus remaining lemon for juice
Salt and pepper
1 tablespoon raw pine nuts
Freshly grated Manchego cheese for garnish

Preheat oven to 400°. Place foil across a small baking sheet. Lay asparagus spears flat, drizzle with olive oil, a squeeze of the lemon juice, and season with salt and pepper. Place lemon slices and sprinkle pine nuts across asparagus. Roast in oven for 15-20 minutes, or until desired doneness. Garnish with freshly grated manchego cheese, serve.

Brussels Sprout Salad

(Serves 3-4)

---

2 tablespoons lemon juice
1 tablespoon Dijon mustard
1 tablespoon shallot, minced finely
4 tablespoons olive oil
1/2 teaspoon salt
1/4 teaspoon pepper
1 pound brussels sprouts grated or chopped finely
1 apple, peeled, cored, and diced (drizzle with some lemon juice to prevent browning)
1/2 cup grated smoked Gouda cheese
1/2 cup toasted pecan pieces

Whisk lemon juice, Dijon mustard, shallot, olive oil, salt, and pepper in a small bowl. Combine brussels sprouts, apple, Gouda, and pecan in a large bowl. Fold dressing into salad and serve.

Brussels Sprout Leek Casserole

(Serves 4-6)

1 bag of brussels sprouts (about 25 sprouts), quartered
1 green apple, peeled, cored, and chopped into chunks
2 leeks, white and pale green parts only, rinsed well, chopped into 1/4-inch pieces
1 cup heavy cream
Salt and pepper to taste

Preheat oven to 400°. Combine brussels sprouts, apple pieces, and leeks in a large bowl to mix.

Spread mixture into a 9 x 12 casserole dish. Pour heavy cream over the mixture. Mix around to coat contents with the cream. Season with salt and pepper.

Bake in oven for 40 minutes, stirring once to prevent burning the edges of the brussels sprouts. Season once more with salt and pepper before serving.

ALMOND FLOUR ONION RINGS

(Serves 3-4)

2 sweet onions, sliced into 1/2-inch rings and separated
2 eggs, beaten in a bowl
1/2-1 cup almond flour
Salt and pepper
Olive oil

Dredge onions in the egg wash, then coat with almond flour. The almond flour might go on pretty chunky, just roll with it.

Heat 1/4-inch of oil in a non-stick pan to high heat. You know the pan is hot enough when a crumb thrown into the oil sizzles. Fry up onion rings in batches, setting on paper towels to drain. Season with salt and pepper.

FRIED OKRA

(Serves 3-4)

---

1 pound okra, cut into 1/4-inch rounds
1 cup almond flour
1 teaspoon sea salt
1/2 teaspoon freshly ground pepper
1 1/2 cups olive oil for frying (or you can use reserved bacon fat)
1/2 teaspoon garlic salt
1/4 teaspoon smoked paprika
Dash of cayenne

Soak the cut okra rounds for 3 minutes in a bowl of cool water. Drain. This will help the okra get a little sticky and hold the almond flour coating better. Pour the almond flour, salt, and pepper into a large freezer bag and blend. Pour in the okra. Shake the okra in the bag to coat.

In a large, deep-sided skillet heat the oil over medium heat until hot, around 325°. Put down lots of paper towels for draining the cooked okra.

Lift the coated okra from the almond flour, shaking loose any excess almond flour. Add to the hot oil in the skillet. Fry for 6-8 minutes, turning to crisp and brown evenly. Remove to the paper towels to drain. Season with additional salt and pepper to taste.

Whisk together garlic salt, smoked paprika, fresh pepper, and dash of cayenne. Season okra to taste with this spice mix.

Green Beans with Caramelized Shallots

(Serves 3-4)

2 tablespoons olive oil
6 mini bell peppers, sliced (or 1 regular red bell pepper)
1 shallot, sliced
1 pound green beans, washed and trimmed
1 teaspoon salt
1/2 teaspoon garlic salt

Heat olive oil on medium high heat in large sauté pan. Cook peppers until soft, about 3-4 minutes. Add in shallots and cook 4-5 minutes until they start to caramelize. Add in green beans. Toss with shallots and olive oil. Sprinkle on salt and garlic salt. Cover, reduce heat to medium low, and let cook/steam for 10-12 minutes, stirring twice during cooking.

Wild Mushroom and Green Bean Casserole

(Serves 8–10)

Casserole Filling
1 ounce dried wild mushrooms, reconstituted, then chopped
1 tablespoon olive oil
1/2 onion, minced
1 package cremini or baby bella mushrooms, chopped
1/2 teaspoon onion powder
1/2 teaspoon garlic powder
1 tablespoon vodka (optional)
1/2 teaspoon black pepper
1 cup chicken broth
1/2 cup heavy cream
1 pound green beans, ends snapped and cut into 2-inch pieces

Fried Shallot Rings
1/2 cup olive oil
3–4 large shallots, sliced into 1/4-inch slices

Preheat oven to 350°.

Reconstitute dried wild mushrooms in 2 cups boiling water, bring to boil 3–4 minutes, cover, turn off heat, and let stand 30 minutes. Remove wild mushrooms, reserving leftover water as mushroom broth.

Heat olive oil in large sauté pan on medium high heat; then cook onions until soft, about 3–5 minutes. Add in chopped cremini mushrooms, onion powder, and garlic powder until browned, cooking an additional 5–8 minutes. Add the wild mushrooms to the sauté pan, cook 5–8 minutes. Pour in vodka, cook 2–3 minutes until alcohol burns off. Add pepper.

Ladle in 2 scoops of mushroom broth (being careful to avoid the settled grit at the bottom of the reserved mushroom broth) and stir into sauté pan.

Ladle in 3 scoops chicken broth. Bring to boil for 3 minutes. Add in 1/2 cup heavy cream, simmer another 3 minutes. Turn off heat. Mix in green beans, season one more time with salt and pepper.

Pour contents into 9 x 12 baking pan. Bake for 30 minutes uncovered. Stir the contents. Place foil over the top and bake another 25 minutes. Remove from oven; add fried shallot rings (see below) to the top of the casserole. Re-foil and bake 5 more minutes.

Fried Shallots

Slice shallots into 1/4-inch pieces and separate into rings. Heat 1/2-inch of olive oil in pan to high heat. Fry shallots 3–4 minutes, being careful not to burn. Remove shallots from oil, let drain on paper towel. Season with salt.

GINGER PEPPER BABY BOK CHOY

(Serves 2)

2-3 baby bok choy heads, washed
2 tablespoons olive oil
1 medium onion, thinly sliced (or use Lime Soaked Onions, p. 181)
1/2 cup chopped mini bell peppers
1 teaspoon freshly grated ginger
Salt and pepper

Cut off and discard the bottom flat stem of the bok choy, then thinly slice the white and green parts into 1/4-inch pieces, using entire head.

On medium high heat, sauté olive oil in a non-stick pan, add onions and peppers, and sauté until soft, about 5 minutes. Add in sliced bok choy and grated ginger, stirring until ingredients are mixed. Season with salt and pepper. Turn heat down to medium-low. Sauté 7-10 minutes, or until bok choy is soft, stirring pan to make sure ginger doesn't stick to pan. Season once more with salt and pepper, then serve.

Red Cabbage and Kale Slaw

(Serves 8-10)

This is a fresh, colorful, flavorful alternative to the typical, overly sweet, soggy store bought cole slaw.

---

2 cups kale, rough stems cut away and discarded
1 red cabbage, de-stemmed, quartered, then shredded on the largest grate of a box grater (yields about 2-3 cups)
1 small shallot, minced (about 1 tablespoon)
1 tablespoon apple cider vinegar
1 tablespoon champagne vinegar or white wine vinegar
1/4 cup mayonnaise
1/4 cup olive oil, plus more for drizzling
Salt and pepper for seasoning
1/2 cup dried sugar free cranberries, currants, cherries, or raisins (optional)

Lay kale leaves on a flat surface, sparsely drizzle with olive oil, and then massage the kale leaves for one minute. Chop the kale leaves finely. In a large bowl, mix prepared kale and red cabbage. In smaller bowl, whisk together a dressing of shallot, apple cider vinegar, champagne vinegar, mayonnaise, and olive oil. Season with salt and pepper to taste. Add dressing to kale and cabbage mixture, tossing to coat evenly. Add in dried fruit pieces if desired, toss. Serve immediately or refrigerate until ready to serve.

GINGER CILANTRO CAULIFLOWER "RICE"

(Serves 2-3)

Several grocery stores now carry bags of pre-grated cauliflower "rice." I suggest you buy 4-5 of them at a time. Saving the step of grating the cauliflower into the perfect rice size is nothing short of genius. If you don't have access to these little baggies of gold, then you can always hand grate a head of cauliflower, or pulse cauliflower in a food processor or Vitamix® to make the "rice" texture.

1 tablespoon olive oil
1 12-ounce bag cauliflower rice, thawed
(or one head of cauliflower, grated into "rice")
2 tablespoons cilantro, finely chopped
1 teaspoon grated ginger
Salt and pepper

Heat olive oil to medium high heat in a sauté pan. Add cauliflower rice, stirring until heated through, about 3 minutes. Stir in the cilantro and ginger, and season with salt and pepper. Cook for 10 minutes, stirring occasionally, being careful not to burn the cauliflower rice. Lower the heat, and let sit for 5-8 minutes before serving, which gives the rice a little crispness.

ROASTED BUTTERNUT SQUASH "RISOTTO"

(Serves 2-4)

When making traditional risotto, you use Arborio rice and slowly ladle in chicken broth, which the rice absorbs to become creamy and smooth. But since we have cauliflower to the rescue yet again, and cauliflower does not have any starch to absorb the chicken broth, less chicken broth and cooking time are required. Use either a food processor or blender to make "rice" out of a head of cauliflower, or buy pre-riced cauliflower in the frozen veggie section (not widely available). If you don't do dairy, feel free to substitute a dairy free cheese or omit altogether.

---

1 butternut squash, peeled and cubed into 1/2-inch pieces (or one 12-ounce bag of pre-cut butternut squash)
2 tablespoons olive oil
Salt and pepper
1 cauliflower head, florets removed (or two 12-ounce bags of pre-cut cauliflower)
1 medium sweet onion, finely chopped

1/2 teaspoon onion powder
1/2 teaspoon garlic powder
2 tablespoons white balsamic vinegar
1 cup chicken broth
1 teaspoon salt
1/2 teaspoon pepper
1 tablespoon cream cheese
1 cup grated parmesan cheese

Preheat oven to 400°. Cover a large baking sheet with foil. Put butternut squash cubes in bowl. Toss with 1 tablespoon of olive oil and season with salt and pepper. Spread evenly on baking sheet. Roast for 15 minutes, then flip the squash pieces gently (they can stick and burn easily). Roast an additional 15 minutes until soft and browned. Remove from oven and let cool. Lightly smash the squash cubes for later mixing.

Cut any remaining stems off cauliflower florets. Place into food processor or blender, and chop until making the cauliflower into the size of large grains of "rice." Do not overdo this step, or else you will have mush!

In a large sauté pan, heat 1 tablespoon olive oil on medium high heat. Sauté chopped onion 10-12 minutes until very soft and translucent. Add cauliflower rice, let rice get coated with olive oil and start to toast, about 2 minutes. Stir in onion powder and garlic powder. Add white balsamic vinegar, letting the rice sizzle, about 2-3 minutes. Pour chicken broth slowly into your risotto, stirring well. Add 1 teaspoon of sea salt and 1/2 teaspoon of pepper. Stir. Lower heat and let simmer 15 minutes, stirring occasionally. Turn off heat, add in the cream cheese and parmesan cheese, and stir thoroughly. Add in the smashed butternut squash cubes and mix thoroughly. Serve immediately with a dusting of parmesan cheese.

Year-round autumnal goodness.

CAULIFLOWER TOTS

(Yields 24–30 tots)

Since cauliflower has become the perfect substitute where we would have previously used rice or potatoes, let's take this all the way and make my favorite childhood comfort food: the tot. Cauliflower tots are a savory low carb indulgence, made mostly of vegetables, but with that perfect crisp exterior and perfect soft interior. If I were fancy, I'd call them Cauliflower Croquettes. But I am not fancy. No, I am not.

These tots can be made dairy free if you substitute vegan cheese. You can also omit the egg if you need to as they hold together fine without one. To "pre-rice" the cauliflower, simply grate it on a box grater or in a food processor until the consistency of rice. Alternatively, purchase bags of pre-cut cauliflower.

4 cups pre-riced cauliflower (equivalent of about 2 heads of cauliflower)
2 tablespoons olive oil for baking sheet
1/4 cup minced onion
2 tablespoons minced red pepper
2 teaspoons minced fresh jalapeño pepper
2 teaspoons cilantro, finely chopped
1/4 cup almond flour
3/4 cup of shredded cheddar jack cheese
1 teaspoon salt
1/2 teaspoon freshly ground pepper
1 egg

Steam pre-riced cauliflower for 10 minutes in a stovetop steamer insert, or microwave in a bag for 4 minutes. Pour onto a clean, dry towel, and press all excess water out. Press one more time for good measure while allowing cauliflower to cool.

Preheat oven to 400°. Prepare a baking sheet with non-stick foil drizzled with olive oil. In a large bowl, mix the cooled cauliflower, onion, red pepper, jalapeño pepper, cilantro, almond flour, cheese, salt, and pepper until evenly blended. Add egg and mix thoroughly.

Form into tot shaped balls. Lay on baking sheet, about 1/2-inch apart. Bake in oven for 20 minutes. Remove from oven, gently flip the tots, and continue baking for 20 more minutes until crispy and golden brown. Serve immediately.

MIMI'S CURRIED "RICE" SALAD

(Serves 3-4)

Summer needs cold salads. Badly. And my mother-in-law is the inventor of the perfect summer rice salad. Instead of rice, we substitute cauliflower rice. Not because we are carb-phobic, but because we like cauliflower. Plus, my mother-in-law is a fine cook. She would never lead us astray.

---

1 head of cauliflower, stems removed and discarded
1 14-ounce can of artichoke hearts
1 red, yellow, or orange bell pepper, chopped
8 pimiento stuffed olives, chopped
1/2 teaspoon curry powder
2 tablespoons mayonnaise
3 tablespoons olive oil
1/2 teaspoon salt
1/4 teaspoon freshly ground pepper

In a food processor or blender, grind cauliflower florets into "rice." Pour into a microwave safe bowl. Microwave on high for 3 minutes. Drain and press the cauliflower rice until dried. Pour into a large mixing bowl. Let cool completely in fridge.

Drain artichoke hearts. Cut and discard top rough 1/4-inch to 1/2-inch of the artichoke hearts, then quarter the remaining soft hearts. Fold in chopped artichoke hearts, bell pepper, and olives into cauliflower rice until mixed. Sprinkle on curry powder, mixing it in.

In a separate small bowl, whisk together mayo, olive oil, salt, and pepper. Pour over salad and fold in well.

Coconut Ginger Chard

(Serves 2)

Easy greens recipes make it easy to get members of your family to eat their greens. Say yes to hints of coconut and ginger, which take the bitterness right out of the chard. In fact, I'd double the recipe if I were you, as this one here only serves two.

---

2 tablespoons olive oil
1/2 an onion, chopped (or you can use Lime Soaked Onions, p.181)
1 tablespoon minced fresh ginger
10-ounce bag of pre-cut rainbow chard, or 1 bunch of chard, chopped
1 cup of coconut milk
1/8 teaspoon red pepper flakes
Salt and pepper for seasoning

Heat olive oil in a large sauté pan to medium high heat and cook onions and ginger for 5 minutes. Add chard, coconut milk, and red pepper flakes. Toss to coat the chard. Season with salt and pepper. Cover and cook for 7–10 minutes. Season again with salt and pepper before serving.

Cheese Soufflé

(Serves 6-8)

---

4 tablespoons butter, plus more for ramekins
2 tablespoons freshly grated parmesan
2 tablespoons coconut flour
1 cup whole milk
1 1/2 cups grated Gruyère cheese
2 tablespoons chives, finely chopped
1/2 teaspoon salt
1/4 teaspoon pepper
4 egg yolks
3 egg whites
Salt and pepper for seasoning

Preheat oven to 400°. Grease 6-8 3-inch deep ramekins with butter, coat the insides with parmesan, place on cookie sheet and refrigerate.

Melt 4 tablespoons of butter in a sauce pan over medium heat, being careful not to burn. Whisk in coconut flour, stirring for one minute. The flour-butter mixture will start to brown. Slowly whisk in milk, and continue to whisk for an additional 2-3 minutes.

Pour liquid mixture into a large bowl, whisk in Gruyère, chives, 1/2 teaspoon salt and 1/4 teaspoon pepper. Whisk in egg yolks. In a separate smaller bowl, beat egg whites until stiff peaks form. Fold back into the main mixture, doing so in parts.

Pour into ramekins evenly, leaving 1/2-inch space from the lip of the ramekin. Run thumb around the edges of the ramekins to create a circular dip between the edge of the ramekin and the top of the cheese mixture. This prevents the soufflé from spilling over the edge while cooking.

Bake in oven on baking sheet for 15 minutes. Reduce oven heat to 375°, and continue baking until puffed and slightly browned on top, about 15 minutes.

GRAIN-FREE EASY BREAD

2 1/2 cups almond flour
1 teaspoon sea salt
1/2 teaspoon baking soda
3 eggs
1 teaspoon apple cider vinegar
Butter, for greasing pan

Preheat oven to 300°. In a large mixing bowl, mix all ingredients well until a thick dough forms. Grease a loaf pan with butter. Press bread dough evenly into loaf pan.

Bake on bottom rack of oven, 45-50 minutes. Remove from oven, let bread cool.

LOW CARB STUFFING

(Serves 4-6)

4 tablespoons butter
1 large onion, chopped
3 celery stalks, chopped
1/2 teaspoon poultry seasoning
1/2 teaspoon dried thyme
1/2 teaspoon dried oregano
1/2 teaspoon dried basil
1/4 teaspoon onion powder
1/4 teaspoon garlic powder
Grain-Free Easy Bread, cubed into 1/2-inch pieces
1-2 cups chicken broth

Preheat oven to 350°. In a large sauté pan on medium high heat, melt 2 tablespoons of the butter. Cook the onion and celery until very soft in the butter. In a small bowl, mix the dry spices together, and then pour into onion and celery. Mix well.

In a large mixing bowl, pour bread cubes, onions, and celery into a bowl and mix. Add in chicken broth 1/2 cup at a time until you reach desired consistency. Fluff with fork, pour into 8 x 8 pan. Melt remaining 2 tablespoons of butter, and drizzle on stuffing. Bake 20-30 minutes, until browned on top.

Avocado, Salmon, and Spinach Salad

(Yields 2 salads)

2 wild caught salmon fillets
Salt and pepper
Olive oil
2 cups baby spinach
1 orange, segmented
1 avocado, peeled, pitted, and sliced

Dressing:
Juice of 1/2 half lime (about 1 tablespoon)
3 tablespoons olive oil

Preheat oven to 375°. Place salmon fillets on a baking sheet, season with salt and pepper, and drizzle with olive oil. Bake 10-12 minutes, or until salmon is almost cooked through, but not overdone. Remove from oven and let cool.

Break up salmon into pieces and place on serving dishes. Toss with spinach, orange segments, and avocado slices. Whisk together the lime juice and olive oil until emulsified. Drizzle over salad and serve.

Grilled Halloumi and Watermelon Salad

(Serves 4-6)

Halloumi cheese is a mild, salty, deliciously firm Mediterranean white cheese, which holds up well to grilling or searing in a pan. Plus, it has a squeaky snap that pairs really well with a melt-in-your-mouth perfectly ripe summer watermelon. Some grocery stores have Halloumi cheese in the summer season, or you can also find it at a Mediterranean or middle eastern specialty market.

---

7 ounces Halloumi cheese, cut into 1x3-inch rectangular slices
1 small watermelon, insides sliced into 1-2 inch pieces
Olive oil and balsamic vinegar for garnish
1/4 cup thinly sliced fresh basil

Heat grill to 500°, grill the Halloumi, 2 minutes per side. Or, if sautéing in a pan, cook on medium high heat for 3-4 minutes per side. Let cool.

Arrange watermelon pieces and Halloumi on platter. Drizzle with olive oil and balsamic vinegar. Sprinkle chopped basil over whole salad.

Rosemary Sweet Potato Hash

(Serves 4)

2 lbs. sweet potatoes or garnet yams, peeled and cut into 1-inch chunks
1 tablespoon olive oil
1/2 sweet onion, chopped
1 red bell pepper, chopped
1 tablespoon rosemary leaves, finely chopped
Salt and pepper

In a large pot of boiling water, boil sweet potato pieces for 10 minutes. Drain, let cool, and lightly dry any excess water with a paper towel.

In a cast iron skillet, heat olive oil to medium high heat. Add onions and peppers and sauté until soft, about 5-8 minutes. Add sweet potato pieces and rosemary, tossing with onions and peppers. Season with salt and pepper.

Cook in pan 20-25 minutes, only stirring every 5-7 minutes so that you can get a brownish crust on the sweet potato pieces. When you stir, be sure to use a flat spatula so that you don't make mashed potatoes out of your hash. Season with salt and pepper before serving.

"THE STACK" GRILLED VEGETABLE SALAD

(Serves 4)

The Stack is a romp in grilled veggie paradise. With hearty vegetables that stand up to a good grilling and topped with Balsamic Dressing, this salad could be a standalone meal. I like to pair it with anything Italian or grilled ... or both. Use the grill pan indoors in the winter and fire up the grill in the summer.

---

1 eggplant, cut into 1/2-inch slices
Salt for sweating eggplant
2 yellow bell peppers, sliced into large sections
2 beefsteak or heirloom tomatoes, cut into 1/2-inch slices
2 zucchini, cut lengthwise into 1/2-inch slices
2 portobello mushrooms, cut lengthwise into 1/2-inch slices
Balsamic Dressing (see p. 169)
Basil leaves for garnish

Preheat oven to 400°. Roast bell pepper pieces until skin blisters and easily peels off. Let peppers cool, then peel off the skin. While the peppers cool, place eggplant slices on paper towels, sprinkle them with salt, and let them "sweat." Prepare your other veggies, and heat grill or grill pan to medium high heat. Brush the grill with olive oil to prevent veggies from sticking. Pat the eggplant pieces dry, then grill eggplant, zucchini, and portobello slices until softened with sear marks, about 4–5 minutes per side. Remove from heat, then stack portobello, bell pepper, zucchini, tomato, and eggplant into a column. Drizzle with Balsamic Dressing and garnish with basil leaves. Serve immediately.

Chapter Five: Sauces, Marinades, Dressings, and Make Your Own

Béchamel Sauce

(Yields 2.5 cups)

---

2 1/4 cups milk
1/2 stick salted butter
1/4 cup arrowroot starch
Pinch of nutmeg
Salt and pepper for seasoning

Heat the milk on medium heat for about 3–4 minutes, until steamed, careful not to scald.

Melt the butter in a pan over medium heat. Whisk in the arrowroot starch. Pour in the heated milk, whisking constantly and making sure all clumps are whisked out. When it starts to boil, lower the heat, season with a pinch of salt, and let simmer gently. Whisk the mixture every 3–5 minutes. If your sauce gets too thick, add in milk, 1 tablespoon at a time. Remove from heat. Add pinch of nutmeg, a twist or two of fresh pepper, and more salt if necessary.

Use Béchamel sauce as the base in gratins and Zucchini Mac & Cheese (see p.133).

Balsamic Dressing

(Dresses a salad for 4)

This is my most basic of salad dressings. You can't go wrong with this one. Over the years, whenever I go to a fancy grocery store or take a foodie road trip to someplace fun like Napa or Italy, I buy all sorts of interesting vinegars. I invite you to mix and match vinegars, experiment with different dried herbs, and even substitute fresh squeezed lemon, lime, or orange juice for the vinegar to change up the flavor. Whenever you need to increase your recipe, or you'd like to make more in advance and store it for the week, make sure you keep your 3-to-1 oil-to-vinegar ratio. Make as much or as little as you want.

3 tablespoons olive oil
1/2 tablespoon balsamic vinegar
1/2 tablespoon red wine vinegar
1 teaspoon Dijon mustard
Sprinkle of garlic salt, salt, pepper, dried oregano, and dried basil

In a small mixing bowl, combine all ingredients, pulverizing the dried herbs in your hand before adding to the dressing. Whisk all ingredients together, toss with salad.

BARBECUE SAUCE

(Yield 1 1/2 cups sauce)

7 dates, pitted and chopped
1/2 cup organic blueberries
1 6-ounce can organic tomato paste
1 cup water
2 tablespoons vinegar of your choice (I use balsamic)
1 tablespoon butter (substitute olive oil to be dairy-free)
1 teaspoon Dijon mustard
1 teaspoon garlic powder
1 teaspoon onion powder
1/2 teaspoon ground pepper
1/2 teaspoon smoked paprika
2 teaspoons salt
1/4 teaspoon cayenne

Put all ingredients in a large sauce pan or Le Creuset pot. Bring heat to a low boil and simmer for about 15-20 minutes. Remove from heat and let cool for 10 minutes, then pulverize entire contents in a Vitamix® or food processor. If sauce is too thick, you can add water, a tablespoon at a time, until desired thickness is achieved.

Homemade Marinara

(Yields 2 cups)

---

2 14-ounce cans diced tomatoes (with NO sugar!!—check the label)
1/2 can tomato paste (again with NO sugar!!)
1 tablespoon olive oil
1 teaspoon minced garlic (about 2-3 cloves)
10 basil leaves, chopped
1 teaspoon of butter
Pinch of salt

Pulse diced tomatoes and half can of paste in the Vitamix® or blender to purée.

Heat olive oil on medium high heat until very hot. Add garlic and basil, cook for 2 minutes, stir.

Add in tomato purée. Bring to a boil. Add in butter and a pinch of salt. Let simmer for 15-20 minutes, tasting and seasoning with additional salt if needed.

HOMEMADE PIZZA SAUCE

(Yields 1 cup)

1 14-ounce can of diced tomatoes
1 garlic clove, minced (or 1/2 teaspoon minced garlic)
5 basil leaves, chopped
1 tablespoon olive oil
2 tablespoons tomato paste
1 teaspoon of butter
Salt and pepper

Pulse tomatoes in food processor or Vitamix® to make smooth.

In saucepan on medium high heat, sauté garlic and basil in olive oil until soft, about 3 minutes. Add puréed tomatoes and tomato paste, stirring until blended. Lower heat and simmer for 10 minutes. Add butter, salt, and pepper for seasoning. Cook additional 5 minutes. Season again to taste and then use on pizza.

Homemade Pesto

(Yields 1 cup)

2 cups basil leaves washed and patted dry
1/4 cup pine nuts (raw or toasted, your preference)
1 teaspoon minced garlic
1/3-1/2 cup olive oil
1/2 cup freshly grated parmesan
Salt and pepper (completely optional, usually the parmesan
will create enough of a salty flavor)

Place the basil leaves, pine nuts, garlic, and olive oil into the food processor. Grind until chopped, about 3-5 pulses. You may need to use a spatula to scrape down the walls halfway through. Add the parmesan, pulse 2-3 more times until the pesto is your desired consistency. Season with salt and pepper if desired.

Garam Masala

garlic powder
onion powder
ginger

1 teaspoon ground cumin
1/2 teaspoon ground coriander
1/2 teaspoon ground cardamom
1/2 teaspoon ground black pepper
+ 1/4 teaspoon ground cinnamon
1/8 teaspoon ground cloves
1/8 teaspoon ground nutmeg

Combine all of the ingredients together, mix thoroughly, and season Chicken Tikka Masala with it. *p. 81*

Homemade Ricotta Cheese

(Yields 1 cup)

Make ricotta cheese whenever you want to have a low carb snack on hand, or to top a salad or pizza with something fresh and delicious.

---

4 cups whole milk
1/2 cup heavy cream
1/2 teaspoon salt
Juice of 1 small/medium lemon (about a tablespoon and a half)

Bring milk, cream, and salt to a boil, stirring with a wooden spoon so it doesn't get too filmy along the sides of the pot. When at a boil, add the lemon juice. Turn heat down to simmer, and stir constantly. Mixture will begin to curd after 3-4 minutes. The curds will look quite tiny and then clump only slightly more.

Pour the curd mixture into a large bowl through cheesecloth laid in a strainer. The liquid will drain through, and the ricotta will form out of the remaining curds. Only strain the cheese curd mixture for 5-10 minutes to avoid the ricotta getting too dry. Cool off ricotta in the fridge until you are ready to eat it.

HOMEMADE TACO SEASONING

(for use per 1 pound of meat)

---

1 tablespoon chili powder
1/4 teaspoon garlic powder
1/4 teaspoon onion powder
1/4 teaspoon dried oregano
1/2 teaspoon smoked paprika
1 1/2 teaspoons cumin
1 teaspoon salt
1/2 teaspoon pepper
Dusting of cayenne powder for spice (optional)

Mix together thoroughly, and use in place of store-bought taco seasoning.

CHIMICHURRI SAUCE

(Yields 1 cup)

---

1 cup packed parsley, minced (about 1 bunch of parsley)
1 1/2 tablespoons fresh oregano, finely chopped
1 1/2 tablespoons fresh garlic, minced
1/4 teaspoon cayenne pepper
1/2 teaspoon salt
2 tablespoons red wine vinegar
1/4 cup olive oil

In a medium mixing bowl, combine the parsley, oregano, and garlic whisking together. Add cayenne pepper, salt, red wine vinegar, and olive oil to the parsley mixture. Mix it together well, and cover it in plastic wrap. Refrigerate the mixture for as long as possible to let the flavors marry. Serve with Skirt Steak Skewers or alongside any grilled meat.

Homemade Mayo

(Yields 3/4 cup)

Maybe it's a southern girl thing, but I like mayo. It's hard to find a sugar free mayo that doesn't have nasty oil at the base of it. So why not make your own? Add in optional garlic at the end, and then you have garlic aioli, which sounds fancy, but it's just mayo with garlic.

Use your homemade mayo alongside grilled meats, roasted veggies, or as the base for creamy dressings. Keep refrigerated (duh), and make a fresh batch every few days. Homemade mayo contains raw egg yolk, so if you're preggers or immune deficient, you might need to stick to the store bought. But if you are not, then enjoy the heck outta this homemade mayo.

1 large egg yolk
2 teaspoons lemon juice
1 teaspoon champagne vinegar or white vinegar
1/2 teaspoon salt
3/4 cup mild olive oil or avocado oil

In a small mixing bowl, using a hand mixer on the high setting, whisk together the egg, lemon juice, vinegar, and salt until creamy. Dropping in a few drops of the oil at a time, keep using the mixer to whisk up the mayo. It will take about 10-12 minutes to mix in all of the oil, bit by bit, while holding the mixer, which is constantly running.

LIME SOAKED ONIONS

(Yields 1 cup)

A very nice lady from Mexico taught me this trick. It takes your onion experience to the next level. Use these onions in several recipes to augment the flavor: Quesadilla Casserole, Ginger Pepper Bok Choy, Coconut Ginger Chard, plus you can use them in marinades, salad dressings, or even as a pizza topping, slow cooker meat topping, or anything that could be spruced up with some zesty onions.

Juice of 7-8 limes
1 large onion, thinly sliced

Pour lime juice into a small mixing bowl. Place onion slices into lime juice, cover well and refrigerate until use, up to three days.

Green Salsa

(Yield 1 1/2 cups)

---

1 pound tomatillos, peeled and washed
1/2 sweet onion, chopped
1 jalapeño pepper, chopped, stems and seeds removed
1/4 cup cilantro leaves
1 4-ounce can fire roasted green chiles

Preheat oven to 450°. Place clean tomatillos on a foil-lined baking sheet. Roast tomatillos for 10 minutes, or until skin starts to blister. Remove from oven. Let cool.

In a food processor or blender, add roasted tomatillos, onion, jalapeño, cilantro, and green chiles. Blend until desired consistency.

Chapter Six: Breakfast

A Word about Eggs

Eggs are a perfect protein. You can prepare them a dozen different ways. You can scramble, poach, fry, hard boil, soft boil, coddle, and use them in an endless array of ways with a boundless amount of ingredients. I love doing a simple scramble in the morning to use up veggies leftover from the night before. You can also do the same thing to make egg cupcakes, which can then be used as snacks later and breakfast the following morning. Make eggs for dinner if you are hard up for a protein because you forgot to go to the store. Do not be afraid to experiment with eggs.

Minnie's Coddled Egg

(Serves 1)

Having Minnie in your corner is like having a smart, kind, beyond talented Mama Bear by your side, ready to laugh with you at any given moment. We like to cry with each other too, but somehow when she's crying it sounds way cooler because she's British. When she taught me how to make coddled eggs, it all started to make sense. Minnie is that person who can do anything—including coddling a mean egg—and you just wanna be along for the ride.

Butter to grease ramekins
1 egg
2 tablespoons heavy cream
1 basil leaf, finely chopped
Salt and pepper for seasoning
1 teaspoon freshly grated parmesan

Preheat oven to 400°. Grease a shallow ramekin with butter. Crack one egg into ramekin, add in heavy cream, basil, and a twist of salt and pepper. Top with fresh parmesan. Place ramekin on a baking sheet to steady the ramekin and avoid any potential bubbling-over messes.

Place baking sheet in oven, cook for 7-10 minutes, or until egg is at desired doneness. I like a medium poached egg, so I let it cook for 8-9 minutes. Remove from oven, let stand for 1-2 minutes.

Smoked Salmon Scramble

(Serves 2)

4 eggs
1 tablespoon heavy cream
Salt and pepper for seasoning
1 teaspoon of butter
2 ounces smoked salmon, cut into 1/4-inch pieces (about a 1/4 cup)
1 teaspoon minced fresh dill, plus more for garnish
1 tablespoon cream cheese (optional)

In a mixing bowl, beat eggs and heavy cream. Season with a pinch of salt and pepper. In a small non-stick sauté pan, heat butter on medium high heat, coating the pan as it melts. Pour beaten egg mixture into the hot pan. Using a soft rubber spatula, scramble the eggs for 1 minute, until they start to stiffen up. Sprinkle on the salmon, dill, and cream cheese. Continue folding the eggs until they are cooked to desired consistency, usually 2-3 minutes more. Garnish with extra dill and serve immediately.

Rise and Shine Scramble

(Serves 2-3)

1 teaspoon butter
1 tablespoon finely chopped shallot
3 mini bell peppers, chopped (or 1/2 red bell pepper)
1/3 cup heirloom grape tomatoes, halved (or you can use cherry tomatoes)
5-7 basil leaves, chopped
4 eggs
1 teaspoon heavy cream
Salt and pepper
1/4 cup grated cheese (Colby jack, parmesan, cheddar, or your choice)

In a non-stick pan, heat butter until bubbly on medium high heat. Sauté shallots and peppers until soft, about 3-4 minutes, being careful not to burn them. Add tomatoes and basil and let cook another 3-4 minutes until soft and basil is fragrant. In a separate bowl, whisk eggs, cream, salt, and pepper until blended. Pour into hot pan over vegetables. Using a spatula, turn the eggs over and over with the vegetables until scrambled to desired doneness. Garnish with grated cheese. Serve immediately.

Prosciutto Spinach Egg Cupcakes

(Yields 6 Muffins)

There could be a million variations on an egg cupcake, depending on what you have in your fridge. I like packing them with veggies, a little meat, and some cheese. Then you can keep them in the fridge for a quick breakfast or snack. They're good cold or hot.

Quick tip—make sure you press or drain any excess water from the veggies you put into your egg cupcakes or else they will become soggy.

1 teaspoon olive oil
3 cups packed fresh spinach
1/2 teaspoon onion powder
3 slices of prosciutto, trimmed of fat, cut into 1/2-inch pieces
6 eggs
1 tablespoon heavy cream
Salt and pepper for seasoning
3/4 cup shredded cheddar
Olive oil spray for muffin tin

Preheat oven to 350°. Heat olive oil in sauté pan on medium high heat. Dump spinach into pan, add onion powder, toss together, and cover and cook until spinach is wilted, about 2 minutes. Remove spinach from pan and set on paper towel to drain. If desired, sauté prosciutto until crispy, and remove from heat.

In a medium bowl beat eggs and heavy cream, then season with fresh pepper and a pinch of salt. Add cheese to eggs and mix well. Spray muffin pan with olive oil spray to prevent sticking. In muffin cups, evenly distribute spinach and prosciutto. Evenly pour the eggs into the muffin cups over the spinach and prosciutto. Cook for 20-25 minutes at 350°. Serve immediately using a dull knife to easily get egg cupcakes out of the muffin pan.

Cocoa Smoothie

(Serves 2)

2 tablespoons unsweetened cocoa powder
1 cup frozen blueberries
1 cup packed fresh spinach
1 tablespoon almond butter
1 cup almond milk

Blend it all together in a blender or Vitamix® and enjoy!

THE MULTI-VITAMIN SHAKE

(Serves 2-3)

I like adding a lot of water to this recipe so that it tastes more like juice than a chunky smoothie, even though it still retains all of the fiber.

5-6 leaves of romaine lettuce
2-3 stalks celery, chopped
1 cup packed spinach
1 apple, core discarded, cut into chunks
1 inch of ginger, peeled and cut into chunks
1/2 cucumber, cut into chunks
Juice of 1 lemon
2 cups of water

Throw all ingredients in Vitamix® or similar blender and blend until smooooooooth.

Vinnie's Energy Shake

(Yields 2 16 ounce smoothies)

There is no one on this earth quite like my friend Vinnie Tortorich. I'm so lucky to have met him, because without him, this cookbook would be non-existent. He claims he can't cook, but he contributed this smoothie recipe, so I think he's on his way to being an expert, if you ask me.

In the screenplay called, "Anna Buys A Vitamix®," this shake recipe was the inciting incident of my Vitamix® purchase. Along with the Paderno Spiralizer, the Vitamix® is one of my all time favorite kitchen purchases. A Vitamix® is not absolutely necessary to make this puppy, but it sure does blend like a dream. Feel free to substitute avocado for the yogurt and/or coconut oil. Add in fresh ginger, mint, even cayenne, whatever you wanna experiment with. Like the "Angriest Trainer" podcast, this smoothie is one giant evolving experiment, which yields fantastic benefits for those taking the journey.

8-10 raw almonds (or walnuts)
1 cup fresh berries
1/2 cup frozen berries
1/4 cup full fat Greek yogurt (or coconut cream for dairy free)
1 tablespoon coconut oil
1 1/2 cups water
2 cups packed spinach or kale
1/2-1 tablespoon heavy cream (optional, for finishing)

Add all above ingredients except the heavy cream to Vitamix® or other similar blender. Blend until smoooooooth, about 90 seconds to 2 minutes. Add heavy cream, if desired, into final 10 seconds of blending. Pour and serve.

DANIELE'S KALE PIÑA COLADA

(Serves 2)

My writing partner and good friend, Daniele Passantino, gave me this recipe. Together we have written two screenplays and about a bajillion treatments. She's wonderful, and I love her, and I am eternally grateful to her for keeping me on task.

1 cup kale (or spinach)
1/2 cup frozen pineapple
4-5 mint leaves
1/4 cup coconut milk
1 cup water
8 almonds (or nut of your choice—macadamia, hazelnut, cashew, etc)

Blend all ingredients in Vitamix® (or similar blender). Add more water if you want it less dense, add more kale if you want it more kale-like.

ANDREA'S GRAIN FREE GRANOLA

(Serves 4-6)

Have you ever met a new friend later in life and considered, "I thought I had already met all my friends by now." And then five minutes after meeting this new friend, you're thinking, "It feels like we've been friends since we were three." That's Andrea, and after you make this delicious Grain Free Granola, you'll probably feel that way about Andrea too. Note: you can find vegetable glycerin in the skin care aisle of natural food stores.

---

1 cup chopped raw almonds
1 cup chopped raw walnuts
1/2 cup pumpkin seeds
1/2 cup sunflower seeds
1/2 cup unsweetened coconut flakes
1 tablespoon cinnamon
1 teaspoon vanilla
2 tablespoons coconut oil
1 tablespoon vegetable glycerin (optional)
2 tablespoons of coconut sugar (optional)

Preheat oven to 400°. Assemble all ingredients in a plastic baggie and shake, shake, shake.

Spread onto a foil-lined baking sheet. Bake for 5 minutes, being careful not to burn.

Let cool for 20 minutes, then serve or store in snack bags.

FLAXSEED PANCAKES

(Serves 2)

1/4 cup flaxseed meal
1/4 cup coconut flour
1/2 cup whole milk
1 tablespoon Greek yogurt
1 egg
1/2 teaspoon vanilla
1/2 teaspoon baking soda
1/4 cup blueberries
1/4 cup walnut pieces
Butter for frying
Heavy whipped cream (optional)

Combine flaxseed meal, coconut flour, milk, yogurt, egg, vanilla, and baking soda in a large mixing bowl. Mix well. Batter will be quite thick.

Heat a generous pat of butter until bubbling and almost browning on medium high heat in a non-stick pan. Using a 1/4-cup measuring cup, scoop batter into pan. Gently press batter down to form a pancake. Let cook until browned on one side, about 3 minutes. Press a few blueberries and walnut pieces into each pancake, then flip the pancake to cook the other side for an additional 1-2 minutes. Repeat with additional butter and remaining batter until finished.

Spread hot pancakes with an additional thin layer of butter or serve with heavy whipped cream.

Orange Coconut Popovers

(Yields 1 dozen popovers)

4 large eggs
1 can of full fat coconut cream (usually 14-ounce size)
2 teaspoons finely grated orange zest
4 tablespoons butter, melted
1/2 cup coconut flour
1/4 heaping teaspoon xanthan gum
1/2 teaspoon baking soda
1/2 teaspoon salt
3-5 tablespoons of water (optional)

Preheat oven to 425°. In a large bowl, whisk the eggs, coconut cream, and orange zest. The coconut cream will come out of the can a little chunky. Don't be alarmed—just keep whisking until smooth. Whisk in 3 tablespoons of the melted butter. In another bowl, whisk the coconut flour, xanthan gum, baking soda and salt until evenly blended. Whisk the wet ingredients into the dry ingredients until only small lumps remain. Add in water to batter 1 tablespoon at a time to moisten as needed.

Brush the cups of a muffin pan with the remaining 1 tablespoon of melted butter. Heat the muffin pan in the oven for 5 minutes so the butter turns a nutty brown. Fill the muffin cups to almost full with batter. Bake popovers for 25-30 minutes, until risen and browned. Serve with butter and eat straightaway!

Bacon Gruyère Popover variation:

For a savory popover, omit the orange zest and instead add:
1/2 cup shredded Gruyère
1/2 cup cooked bacon, broken into bits

Assemble popovers as indicated above, except omitting the orange zest. After pouring batter into muffin cups, sprinkle the bacon bits and Gruyère on top of each popover. Bake 25-30 minutes until risen and browned, being careful not to overcook the bacon bits on top.

APPLE SPICE MUFFINS

(Makes 6 Muffins)

1 cup ground flax seed meal
1/4 cup coconut flour
1 teaspoon baking soda
1 teaspoon salt
2 tablespoons cinnamon
2 teaspoons ground ginger
1 teaspoon allspice
1/2 teaspoon ground cloves
1/2 teaspoon nutmeg
1 tablespoon coconut oil, melted
2 gala apples, peeled and grated
2 eggs
1/2 cup milk
Spray coconut oil for muffin tin

Preheat oven to 350°. Combine all the dry ingredients and whisk thoroughly. Add in coconut oil, apple, eggs, and milk and mix until combined. Oil a muffin tin, and add batter evenly to the cups. Bake for 35-40 minutes or until a toothpick comes out clean.

Chapter Seven: Desserts

A Word about Sweets

What follows in this chapter is a very humble set of recipes that are intended to help you put life into living. Sugar and grain temptations are everywhere in this world. Take matters into your own hands by making homemade treats from scratch with fresh ingredients.

Each recipe contains very little sugar ratio as compared with the fat in the entire recipe. And you might not recognize some of the sweeteners, but they will become good friends that you only visit with on special occasions as sugary desserts become less and less of a thing.

After a few weeks of eating without sugars and grains, these dessert recipes will taste decadent, and I promise you will never miss a grocery store sheet cake ever again.

ALMOND BUTTER CUPS

(Yields 6)

1/3 cup coconut oil, melted
2/3 cup almond butter
1 teaspoon vanilla extract
2 ounces 85% cacao dark chocolate (optional)

Whisk together all ingredients except chocolate. Fill muffin tins halfway until you've used up the batter. Put in fridge until hardened, at least 2 hours, then pop out of muffin tin. Keep refrigerated prior to eating so the almond butter cups keep their form.

Melt chocolate in double broiler or microwave. Pour chocolate into a small plastic baggie, forcing chocolate down into one corner of the bag bottom. Snip the corner with scissors and drizzle chocolate over the top of the almond butter cups. Place cups back into fridge for chocolate to harden.

Sautéed Berries with Mint Whipped Cream

(Serves 4)

3 cups strawberries
Juice of 1/2 lemon
1 teaspoon lemon or orange zest
1 tablespoon water
8 ounces heavy whipping cream
5 mint leaves, finely chopped

Remove and discard caps from strawberries. Cut strawberries into bite-sized pieces. In a large sauté pan on medium high heat, add strawberries, lemon juice, zest, and water. Cook until the berries get soft and aromatic, about 3-4 minutes. Remove from heat.

In a cold metal bowl, whip the heavy cream and mint pieces until a firm consistency. Serve the sautéed berries topped with the mint whipped cream.

Mixed Berry Clafouti

(Serves 4)

Butter at room temperature for greasing the baking dish
2 cups coarsely chopped berries
1/4 cup coconut sugar
3 tablespoons coconut flour
1/2 teaspoon salt
2 eggs
1 1/4 cup heavy cream, divided
3/4 cup whole milk
Zest of one lemon, finely chopped (about 1 teaspoon)

Preheat oven to 400°. Generously butter an 8 x 8 baking dish. Scatter loosely chopped mixed berries into dish.

Mix together coconut sugar, coconut flour, and salt in mixing bowl. Whisk in eggs, one at a time, then 3/4 cup of the heavy cream, the milk, and the lemon zest. Pour mixed wet ingredients over berries in dish evenly.

Bake for 40-45 minutes, until puffed and brown around edges. The liquid should be cooked through. Let cool. Clafouti will sink in the middle. Whip the remaining 1/2 cup heavy cream to soft peaks. Serve clafouti lukewarm or cooled, topped with whipped cream.

CHEESECAKE TART

(Serves 6-8)

For the pie crust:
1 cup almond flour
1/4 cup coconut flour
1 stick salted butter, melted

Preheat oven to 350°, combine almond flour, coconut flour, and melted butter into a mixing bowl until evenly mixed and a dough forms. Press evenly into spring form pan. Bake 15-20 minutes or until golden brown. Then let it cool.

For the cheesecake tart filling:
1 pack cream cheese at room temperature
1 1/2 teaspoons vanilla
1/2 cup coconut sugar
Pinch of salt
1/2 cup full fat Greek yogurt
1/2 cup heavy cream, whipped

Whip cream cheese until fluffy. Whip in vanilla extract, coconut sugar, salt, and Greek yogurt until blended. Fold in the whipped cream. Pour into the cooled pie crust and refrigerate for 8 hours or overnight.

For the berry topping:
2 cups strawberries, quartered
2 tablespoons balsamic vinegar

Pour balsamic over strawberries and mix gently with a spatula until strawberries are coated with balsamic. Let sit for 5-10 minutes for the strawberries to absorb the balsamic. Top cheesecake tart evenly with the balsamic strawberries.

OR
2 cups fresh raspberries and blueberries

Evenly top the cheesecake tart with a layer of fresh blueberries and raspberries

Lemon Cake

(Serves 6-8)

CAKE
2 cups almond flour
1/2 cup coconut flour
1/2 teaspoon sea salt
3 teaspoons baking powder
1/2 cup raw honey, warmed to liquid if it is a solid
2/3 cup coconut oil, warmed to liquid if it is solid (plus additional to grease pan)
5 eggs
3/4 cup coconut cream
2 tablespoons vanilla extract
1 tablespoon finely chopped lemon zest

GLAZE
Juice of 2-3 lemons
Zest of 1 lemon
1/4 cup raw honey
1 vanilla bean pod

Preheat oven to 350°. Lightly grease an 8 x 8 inch cake pan with coconut oil. After the pan is oiled, fit parchment paper to the bottom of the pan. Combine almond flour, coconut flour, sea salt, and baking powder in a large mixing bowl. Stir the ingredients together with a whisk making sure to break apart any lumps. Using either a blender, food processor, or hand mixer, combine the honey and coconut oil. Blend together for 1-2 minutes. Then add the eggs, one at a time. Finally, add the coconut cream, vanilla extract, and lemon zest. Once all of the wet ingredients are thoroughly combined, pour them into the bowl with the dry ingredients. Mix together with a whisk until all lumps have been removed. Then pour the cake mixture into the cake pan. Bake for approximately 35 minutes, or until a toothpick inserted into the center comes out clean.

While the cake is baking, prepare the glaze. In a small saucepan over medium high heat, combine the lemon juice, lemon zest, and honey. Cut the vanilla bean pod lengthwise and scrape out the beans into the saucepan. Add the bean pods. Reduce heat and simmer for 10–15 minutes, stirring occasionally, until a glaze forms, being careful not to burn. Remove from heat and discard bean pods.

When the cake is finished, allow it to stand for at least 10 minutes before you attempt to remove it from the pan. Run a knife along the sides of the cake to loosen it from the pan. Remove the cake to a serving platter.

Using a fork, pierce the top of the cake several times so that when you pour the glaze over it, the cake will absorb more of the glaze. Use a spatula to evenly spread the glaze around. Once glazed, allow the cake to sit for at least an hour before serving so the glaze flavor becomes fully absorbed. Serve or store in the fridge to serve later.

Sautéed Peaches with Cinnamon Almond Cookie Crumble

(Serves 2)

1 tablespoon butter
3 peaches peeled, pitted, and sliced
1 teaspoon vanilla
1 1/2 cups almond flour
2 tablespoons maple syrup
1 egg
1 tablespoon cinnamon
1 cup heavy whipping cream, whipped, for garnish

Preheat oven to 350°. In a large sauté pan, melt the butter on medium high heat. Add peach slices and vanilla, cooking 3–4 minutes per side, until soft. Remove from heat.

In a large mixing bowl, combine almond flour, maple syrup, egg, and cinnamon into a cookie dough. On a foil-lined baking sheet, press the dough to a 1/2-inch thick cookie, then bake for 15 minutes until golden around the edges. Remove from oven and let cool 10 minutes before breaking apart into cookie crumbles.

Divide peaches into individual ramekins, top with cookie crumbles and a dollop of fresh heavy whipping cream.

PALEO PUMPKIN PIE

(Serves 8)

Guilt free pie, can you even imagine?

This recipe has half the sugar of a traditional pumpkin pie, and I promise you won't miss it. Also, it is completely grain free and uses organic coconut sugar, which makes it a paleo darling. To make it perfectly paleo, substitute coconut cream for the heavy cream and coconut oil for the butter.

Crust:
2 cups almond flour
1 stick salted butter, melted (or substitute coconut oil if avoiding dairy)
1 teaspoon coconut sugar
1 teaspoon cinnamon

Preheat oven to 350°. Combine all ingredients together, mixing well. Press into a 9-inch pie pan evenly. Bake for 20 minutes until golden brown.

Filling:
3 eggs
1 cup heavy cream, plus 1 cup for whipped topping garnish
(or substitute coconut cream for truly paleo)
1 teaspoon vanilla
1 15-ounce can organic pumpkin
3/4 cup coconut sugar
1 tablespoon maple syrup
2 tablespoons ground cinnamon
2 teaspoons ground ginger
1 teaspoon allspice
1/2 teaspoon ground cloves
Pinch of salt

Preheat oven to 350°. Make the crust above.

In a large bowl, lightly beat the eggs. Add in 1 cup of the heavy cream along with the vanilla, pumpkin, coconut sugar, and maple syrup and whisk together. In a small bowl, mix the cinnamon, ginger, allspice, ground cloves, and pinch of salt. Whisk spice mixture into wet ingredients.

Pour filling into crust, bake for 30-35 minutes. The custard will still be jiggly in the middle, so turn the oven down to 325° and cook for the remaining 15-20 minutes. Place foil around the edges of your pie if you find the crust is getting a little too done.

Top with fresh whipped cream.

Chocolate Coconut Chia Pudding

(Serves 4-6)

Sometimes you need a little sweet. This deliciously smooth and easy to make pudding requires just a touch of coconut sugar to send it over the edge of decadence—but all that fat from the coconut cream lowers the glycemic load.

---

1 can full fat coconut cream
3 tablespoons cocoa powder
2 tablespoons coconut sugar
1/2 cup chia seeds
1/2 cup coconut milk or whole milk
1/2 cup heavy cream, whipped for garnish (optional)
1/4 cup raspberries for garnish (optional)

Whisk all of the ingredients together until smooth and well blended. Divide and place into ramekins or small bowls. Put in fridge and let set for at least 3 hours. Garnish with whipped cream and berries.

Vanilla Panna Cotta

(Serves 6-8)

Nonstick cooking spray
3 1/2 teaspoons unflavored gelatin
1/3 cup water
2 cups heavy whipping cream
1/3 cup coconut sugar
1 vanilla bean
2 cups whole milk

Lightly coat 6-8 custard cups (the size of the cups will determine how many you need) or ramekins with non-stick spray. Place in pan and set aside. In a small bowl, sprinkle gelatin over water. Do not stir, and let stand for 5 minutes.

In a saucepan combine heavy whipping cream and sugar. Cut vanilla bean lengthwise and scrape seeds into saucepan with cream and sugar. Once you've scraped all of the seeds in, throw the pod in there, too. Heat until hot, but not boiling. Add the gelatin mixture, and stir until dissolved. Give the vanilla bean one final scrape, and remove it from the pan. Turn off the heat and whisk in the whole milk. Pour the mixture into the custard cups and put in the fridge for at least 4 hours, and up to 24 hours before serving.

Pumpkin Walnut Cookies

(Yield 16-18 cookies)

---

1 cup puréed pumpkin
1 cup almond flour
1/2 cup coconut cream
1/2 cup walnuts, finely chopped
3 tablespoons maple syrup
1 tablespoon cinnamon
1 teaspoon baking powder
1/2 teaspoon salt
1 egg
Coconut oil to grease the baking sheet

Preheat oven to 375°. In a large mixing bowl combine pumpkin, almond flour, coconut cream, walnuts, maple syrup, cinnamon, baking powder, and salt. Whisk together until mixed well. Whisk in the egg, mixing well. Grease a baking pan with coconut oil, and using a tablespoon, drop heaping scoops of batter onto baking sheet, spaced at least 1 inch apart. Bake for 25-30 minutes, until crisp on the outside and cakey on the inside. Let cookies stand 5-10 minutes on baking sheet before serving.

Mexican Chocolate Pots

(Serves 4)

4 egg yolks
3 tablespoons coconut sugar
1 1/4 cups whole milk
1/2 cup heavy cream
1 tablespoon plus 1 teaspoon cinnamon
1 teaspoon vanilla extract
8 ounces 85% cacao dark chocolate, finely chopped
Heavy cream, whipped for serving

In a medium mixing bowl, whisk together egg yolks and coconut sugar. In a sauce pan on medium high heat, bring milk and heavy cream to a boil. Remove from heat. Slowly whisk the milk and cream into the egg mixture, whisking constantly. Then pour the entire liquid back into the saucepan. Place back on heat, and whisk in cinnamon and vanilla, then continue to whisk constantly for 2-3 minutes until a custard forms. Remove saucepan from heat, whisk in the chocolate and keep stirring until melted and a creamy pudding forms.

Pour into 4 small ramekins and refrigerate for 4-6 hours or overnight. Serve with whipped cream.

STRAWBERRY "ICE CREAM" WITH DARK CHOCOLATE CHIPS

(Serves 3-4)

3 cups frozen strawberries
1/2 cup of heavy cream
1 ounce (2 small squares) 85% cacao dark chocolate—
chopped into chip-sized pieces

In Vitamix® or blender, blend strawberries and heavy cream for 2 to 2 1/2 minutes or until blended well. You may need to stop blending to scrape down the sides or use the Vitamix® smasher during blending. The "ice cream" will be a nice shade of pink. Remove strawberry and cream mixture from blender and transfer into a bowl. Fold in dark chocolate pieces. Cover and put in freezer for 10-15 minutes so it hardens up a little bit. Scoop into bowls and serve immediately.

Eat Happy Recipe Index

Cheese Biscuits/Cheese Straws, 14

Cheesecake Tart, 211

Cheese Crisps, 8

Cheese Soufflé, 157

Cheese Stuffed Mini Peppers, 17

Cheesy Zucchini Bake, 110

Chicken Dijon, 79

Chicken Parm, 73

Chicken Queso Dip, 22

Chicken Sage Soup, 117

Chicken Tikka Masala, 81

Chicken with Artichokes, Spinach, and Cherry Tomatoes, 76

Chili Lime Flat Iron Steak, 43

Chimichurri Sauce, 179

Chocolate Coconut Chia Pudding, 218

Cocoa Smoothie, 191

Coconut Crusted Shrimp, 42

Coconut Ginger Chard, 156

Creamed Spinach, 137

Daniele's Kale Piña Colada, 195

Deviled Eggs with Greek Yogurt, 16

Easiest Roasted Chicken Ever, 71

Easy Turkey Burgers, 90

Eggplant Parmesan Casserole, 112

Fall Off the Bone BBQ Ribs, 107

Fancy Turkey Burgers, 89

Fast(er) Carnitas, 68

Flamenquines, 63

Lemony Chicken Thighs, 83

Lemony Spinach, 135

Lentil Burgers with Zestified Greek Yogurt, 95

Lime Soaked Onions, 181

Low Carb Stuffing, 159

Low Carb Vichyssoise, 116

Machaca, 53

Mango Salsa, 23

Mexican Chocolate Pots, 223

Mimi's Curried "Rice" Salad, 154

Minnie's Coddled Egg, 184

Mixed Berry Clafouti, 209

Moroccan Chicken Stuffed Acorn Squash, 87

Nonni's Broccolini, 129

Orange Coconut Popovers, 200

Orange Ginger Pork Chops, 64

Paleo Pumpkin Pie, 216

Pan Fried Bone-In Rib Eye, 47

Pistachio Crusted Coriander Salmon, 35

Pittsburgh Turkey Chili, 99

Pork Chili Verde, 109

Pork Chop Dry Rub, 60

Pork Scaloppini, 65

Pork Tenderloin Medallions, 61

Prosciutto Spinach Egg Cupcakes, 188

Prosciutto Wrapped Peaches, 7

Pulled Pork BBQ, 108

Pumpkin Walnut Cookies, 222

Eat Happy Ingredient Index

Yogurt

Tzatziki Dip, 9

Deviled Eggs with Greek Yogurt, 16

Lentil Burgers with Zestified Greek Yogurt, 95

Zucchini

Zucchini Pasta Bolognese, 59

Cheesy Zucchini Bake, 110

Sausage Zucchini Bake, 111

Lemon Oregano Zucchini Pasta with Cauliflower, 130

Spicy Zucchini Pasta with Pesto, 131

Zucchini Béchamel Mac & Cheese, 133

Zucchini Dijon Sauté, 134

"The Stack" Grilled Vegetable Salad, 165